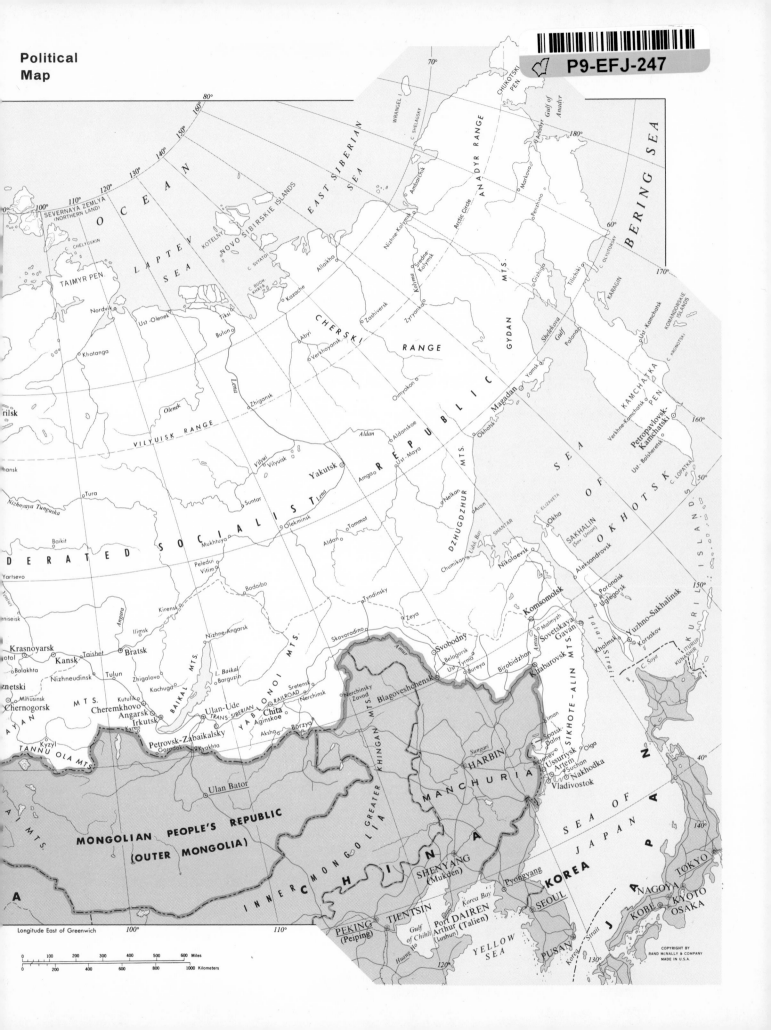

## Political
## Map

P9-EFJ-247

SEVERNAYA ZEMLYA
(NORTHERN LAND)

O C E A N

TAIMYR PEN.

C. CHELYUSKIN

Nordvik

Khatanga

Ust-Olenek

Tiksi

Bulun

Olenek

VILYUISK RANGE

Zhigansk

L A P T E V

S E A

KOTELNY

NOVO SIBIRSKIE ISLANDS

C. SVYATOI

Kazache

Abyi

Verkhoyansk

Allaikha

E A S T - S I B E R I A N

S E A

WRANGEL I

C. SHELAGSKY

Nizhne-Kolymsk

Srednre-
Kolymsk

Zashiversk

Zyryanka

CHUKOTSKI
PEN.

Ambarchik

Arctic Circle

Penzhino

70°

180°

A N A D Y R   R A N G E

Markovo

Gulf of Anadyr

Anadyr

60°

B E R I N G

S E A

170°

C H E R S K I

R A N G E

Oimyakon

Aldan

G Y D A N

Gizhiga

C. OLYUTORSKY

KARAGIN

KOMANDORSKIE
ISLANDS

Nizhnyaya Tunguska

Tura

Olenek

VILYUISK RANGE

Vilyui

Vilyuisk

Suntar

Yakutsk

Lena

Amga

Aldan

Ust-Maya

S O C I A L I S T

R E P U B L I C

M T S.

Yams

Shelekova Gulf

Palana

K A M C H A T K A   P E N.

Verkhne-Kamchatsk

Petropavlovsk-
Kamchatski

160°

Baikit

Yartsevo

Yenisei

Peledui

Vitim

Bodaibo

Mukhtuya

Olekminsk

Aldan

Tommot

Nelkan

Ayon

DZHUGDZHUR MTS.

Magadan

Okhotsk

Udsk Bay

Ulia Bay

Chumikan

Nikolaevsk

C. ELIZAVETA

Okha

SHANTAR

S E A

O F

O K H O T S K

Aleksandrovsk

Poronaisk

Uglegorsk

Ust-Bolsheretsk

C. LOPATKA

50°

K U R I L   I S L A N D S

C. KRONOTSKI

150°

Krasnoyarsk

Kansk

Balakhta

Nizhneudinsk

Taishet

Bratsk

Tulun

Zhigalovo

Kachuga

Kirensk

Nizhne-Angarsk

Ilimsk

Angara

BAIKAL MTS.

L. Baikal

Barguzin

Jyndinsky

Zeya

Skovorodino

Svobodny

Belogorsk

Ust-Tyrma

Bureya

Birobidzhan

Komsomolsk

Malmyzh

Amur

Sovetskaya
Gavan

Kholmsk

Korsakov

Yuzhno-Sakhalinsk

SAKHALIN
(Sov. Union)

Tatar Strait

ITURUP

KUNASHIR

C. SOYA

40°

Minusinsk

Chernogorsk

Kyzyl

TANNU OLA MTS.

AYAN

MTS.

Kutulik

Cheremkhovo

Angarsk

Irkutsk

Kyren

Petrovsk-Zabaikalsky

Gorodok

Kyakhta

Ulan-Ude

TRANS-SIBERIAN

Chita

Aginskoe

Aksha

Borzya

Y A B L O N O I   M T S.

Sretensk

Nerchinsk

Nerchinsky
Zavod

Blagoveshchensk

RAILROAD

K H I N G A N   M T S.

G R E A T E R

Sungari

HARBIN

M A N C H U R I A

Amur

Iman

Spassk-
Dolny

Ussuriysk

Artem

Suchan

Vladivostok

Nakhodka

Olga

S I K H O T E - A L I N   M T S.

S E A

O F

J A P A N

Ulan Bator

M O N G O L I A N   P E O P L E ' S   R E P U B L I C

(O U T E R   M O N G O L I A)

AI MTS.

A

I N N E R   M O N G O L I A

C H I N A

SHENYANG
(Mukden)

Pyongyang

SEOUL

K O R E A

Korea Bay

PEKING
(Peiping)

TIENTSIN

Gulf
of Chihli

Port
Arthur
(Lushun)

DAIREN
(Talien)

Huang Ho

Y E L L O W

S E A

PUSAN

Korea Strait

130°

J A P A N

NAGOYA

KOBE

OSAKA

KYOTO

TOKYO

140°

0  100  200  300  400  500  600 Miles

0  200  400  600  800  1000 Kilometers

COPYRIGHT BY
RAND McNALLY & COMPANY
MADE IN U.S.A.

LIFE WORLD LIBRARY
# RUSSIA

TIME LIFE BOOKS

LIFE WORLD LIBRARY
LIFE NATURE LIBRARY
LIFE SCIENCE LIBRARY
THE LIFE HISTORY OF THE UNITED STATES
GREAT AGES OF MAN
TIME-LIFE LIBRARY OF ART
TIME READING PROGRAM
INTERNATIONAL BOOK SOCIETY

LIFE Pictorial Atlas of the World
The Epic of Man
The Wonders of Life on Earth
The World We Live In
The World's Great Religions
The LIFE Book of Christmas
LIFE's Picture History of Western Man
The LIFE Treasury of American Folklore
America's Arts and Skills
300 Years of American Painting
The Second World War
LIFE's Picture History of World War II
Picture Cook Book
LIFE Guide to Paris

# Introduction

It is not easy for people in a democracy to take a realistic view of any country they have come to regard as "the enemy." The tendency is to disregard all the specific peculiarities of such a country, to equate it with any and every other enemy, to credit its leaders with diabolic intent and efficiency, and to let it go at that. Democracies have often damaged their own interests by this tendency to dehumanize the adversary and to oversimplify his personality.

The Soviet Union presents a special problem. For many years its leaders have brought to the institutions and aspirations of our people a prejudice and an ill will unequaled in our historical experience except by the hostility more recently directed toward us by the Chinese Communists. Russian and American armies, God be thanked, have never fought each other on any significant scale, but never have rulers of another country succeeded in establishing themselves more firmly as "the enemy" in the eyes of the American people than have the leaders of the Soviet Union through the anti-American policies and propaganda of several decades. Yet this hostility has never been total; it has always been complicated by contrary impulses; and in recent years it has undergone and is still undergoing important modifications.

Two great dangers now present themselves. One is that we fail to recognize the extent and significance of the changes that have occurred since Stalin's death, and therefore hope for too little. The other is that we fail to recognize the extent to which Soviet policy is still burdened not only by ideological prejudice but by habits of mind and reflexes inherited from Russia's dark historical past, and that we therefore hope for too much. Either extreme can hold great dangers, for our national security may well depend in coming years on our ability to see Russia realistically. Whoever reads carefully Mr. Charles Thayer's interpretive text and ponders the significance of the illustrations in this volume should find himself fortified in both directions.

GEORGE F. KENNAN
*former U.S. Ambassador to the Soviet Union*

## TIME-LIFE BOOKS

EDITOR
Norman P. Ross
EXECUTIVE EDITOR
Maitland A. Edey
TEXT DIRECTOR     ART DIRECTOR
Jerry Korn     Edward A. Hamilton
CHIEF OF RESEARCH
Beatrice T. Dobie
*Assistant Text Director:* Harold C. Field
*Assistant Art Director:* Arnold C. Holeywell
*Assistant Chiefs of Research:*
Monica O. Horne, Martha Turner

•

PUBLISHER
Rhett Austell
*General Manager:* Joseph C. Hazen Jr.
*Planning Director:* Frank M. White
*Business Manager:* John D. McSweeney
*Circulation Manager:* Joan D. Manley
*Publishing Board:* Nicholas Benton, Louis Bronzo,
James Wendell Forbes, John S. Wiseman

## LIFE MAGAZINE

EDITOR: Edward K. Thompson
MANAGING EDITOR: George P. Hunt
PUBLISHER: Jerome S. Hardy

LIFE WORLD LIBRARY

SERIES EDITOR: Oliver E. Allen
Editorial Staff for *Russia:*
*Assistant Editor:* Jay Brennan
*Designer:* Ben Schultz
*Chief Researcher:* Elizabeth Hawley
*Researchers:* Albert Beryl Hudes, Elizabeth K. Valkenier,
Patricia Appel, Renée Pickèl, Sondra Albert,
Paula von Haimberger Arno, Evelyn Hauptman, Louise Samuels

EDITORIAL PRODUCTION
*Color Director:* Robert L. Young
*Copy Staff:* Marian Gordon Goldman, Patricia Miller,
Dolores A. Littles
*Picture Bureau:* Margaret K. Goldsmith
*Art Assistants:* Douglas B. Graham, John M. Woods

The text for the chapters of this book was written by Charles W. Thayer. Valuable help was provided by these individuals and departments of Time Inc.: Stan Wayman, Carl Mydans, John Dominis and Leonard McCombe, LIFE staff photographers; Doris O'Neil, Chief, LIFE Picture Library; Richard M. Clurman, Chief, TIME-LIFE News Service; Peter Draz, Chief, Bureau of Editorial Reference.

# Contents

COVER: The 15th Century
red brick walls of the Kremlin (*left*),
seat of power in Russia, overlook
Red Square and the many-domed
St. Basil's Cathedral, today a museum.

## ABOUT THE WRITER

Charles W. Thayer, a 1933 graduate of the U.S. Military Academy who switched to the diplomatic field, began acquiring his special knowledge of Russia and its people when he served in the American Embassy in Moscow from 1933 to 1937. His experiences at that time, and in subsequent visits to the Soviet Union during his two decades in the foreign service, form the basis for the interpretive text by him in this volume. In 1953 Thayer resigned from the foreign service to take up writing full time, and he has since become known both for his insight into Soviet policies and for his penetrating observations on the diplomatic world. His books include *Bears in the Caviar*, *The Unquiet Germans*, *Diplomat* and *Moscow Interlude*.

*Russia* © 1960, 1963, 1965 Time Inc. All rights reserved.
Published simultaneously in Canada.
Library of Congress catalogue card number 61-12369.
School and library distribution by Silver Burdett Company.

LIFE WORLD LIBRARY

# RUSSIA

by Charles W. Thayer

and The Editors of LIFE

TIME INCORPORATED    NEW YORK

CELEBRATING, Soviet citizens throng Red Square in 1961 to cheer Yuri Gagarin, who was the first human to orbit the earth. His pictures are in the background.

# 1

# Stage Setting for a Stormy Empire

IN its history, its size and its complexity Russia is a world of its own. An American goes "over" to England or France. An Englishman goes "up" to London or "across" to Paris. But the visitor goes "in" to that sprawling land known as Russia but more correctly called the Soviet Union or the Union of Soviet Socialist Republics (U.S.S.R.). Yet were it not for the stern police and earnest customs guards at the border it would be difficult to know just when you had entered the country. The frontiers of Russia—to use the land's traditional name—have shifted westward or eastward roughly a dozen times in the past half century. Officially the western frontier today is at Brest-Litovsk, where in 1918 Russia made peace with Germany, but Soviet troops also stand guard on the Elbe, 500 miles across Poland and East Germany.

Nor will the landscape provide a clue even if you renounce the convenience of a plane for the slower but more revealing journey by railroad. Some European travelers maintain that Russia begins at Berlin's East Station, for once the outskirts of the city have been passed the countryside becomes flat and scrubby. Forests of birch trees alternate with pastures and cultivated fields. Instead of the neat, painted and compact villages typical of Western Europe, straggling clusters of wooden houses appear along broad cobblestone roads. Instead of trim gardens, a few sunflowers adorn the front yards.

AS you move farther "in" through Poland the paint on the wooden huts fades until the log walls are bare and gray. The cultivated fields give way to swamps, and the birch forests, with their clusters of diminutive white-trunked trees, stretch interminably across the landscape. On and on the train rattles across the gently rolling countryside of European Russia (the country's western section), beyond the Pripet Marshes where Russian armies have traditionally defended their frontiers against invaders from Europe.

From time to time a tractor breaks the monotony of the motionless, featureless countryside, its plump girl driver wrapped in shawls so that only her fat red cheeks and wide eyes are visible. Perhaps a bearded, rubber-booted peasant prods a scrawny horse harnessed by a high yoke to a cart or sledge.

The unfenced fields and pastures of European Russia stretch to the distant horizon—and far beyond across the rich, rolling plains, or "steppes," of the Ukraine to the Black Sea in the south, and across the endless forests and swamps to the Gulf of Finland and the Barents Sea in the north.

Only after long hours will the traveler see the first of the many rings that encircle Moscow, the mecca not only of all Russians but of much of the Communist world. This circle is the *dacha* suburb where the better-off Muscovites own or rent country homes, while their less well-to-do neighbors, who are not permitted to move into overcrowded Moscow, live in less pretentious homes.

In the distance are the high, gray spires of Stalin's skyscrapers, rising above the cupolas from which Moscow once got its name as "The City of Forty Times Forty Churches." Inside the Byelorussian Station, the terminal from the west, you get your first pungent whiff of Russia: human sweat and the rancid smell of black bread. Every bench is crowded with shawled farm women and rubber-booted men, their bundles and boxes piled around them.

Presently you emerge on the wide black boulevards that run in all directions from the Kremlin, strips of black asphalt often 100 feet wide, jammed with open trucks spurting out black clouds of exhaust, droves of small taxis and limousines in which a high official sits beside the driver to emphasize his democratic attitude. Many of the automobiles are quite new.

Along the narrow sidewalks on either side of the boulevard, streams of pedestrians hurry to and from work, darting into shops to buy groceries or pausing for a few seconds to admire a window display. Their faces are stolid and expressionless, like those of any busy urban crowd. Most of the people are plainly but adequately dressed, the men generally in dark shades. But many of the women seek more color: print dresses, colorful scarves and hats in various shades from magenta to aquamarine.

THE true Russians among them are distinguished by their round, flat faces, their high cheekbones and wide eyes, and their wide mouths which in moments of relaxation can stretch from ear to ear in laughter. But Moscow crowds are composed of many races. There are lean, mustached, dark-eyed Georgians or Armenians, flat-faced Mongols from Asian sections of Russia, black visitors from Africa and ascetic, thin, olive-skinned Indians.

Scurrying in and out of the crowds are groups of school children, the boys wearing the red kerchief that is the insignia of the Pioneers, the Communist children's organization; the pig-tailed girls in pinafores with clean white collars. Spotting a foreigner, the youngsters crowd around to ask for chewing gum, which is not made in Russia. But if the uncomprehending foreigner thinks that they are begging and tosses them some Russian money they will indignantly throw it back to him. Beggars are not seen on Moscow's streets. Only on the steps of churches are they to be found, tattered remnants of ancient Moscow—the Moscow of the czars and priests.

THOUGH Moscow is indeed ancient, it is not the oldest city of Russia. That honor belongs to Kiev, now the provincial capital of the Ukraine but once the center of a vast realm that reached as far as the Volga River in the northeast. It was in Kiev that Russia's last pagan ruler, Vladimir I, was baptized in the 10th Century and from which he requested the Patriarch of Constantinople to send out missionaries to Christianize his subjects. The rulers of Kiev dominated Russia for almost 300 years, but at the end of the 12th Century their leadership passed to princes in the north and eventually to the Muscovites.

Moscow itself originated as a small settlement on the banks of the Moskva River. In the mid-12th Century it was encircled by a wall, and in the following century Daniel Nevski, son of Prince Alexander Nevski, Grand Duke of Kiev, founded the principality of Muscovy, the nucleus from which the U.S.S.R. of today has grown. From then until the present day the city of Moscow has expanded in spasmodic leaps to keep pace with the empire of which it has been the center—if not always the capital.

Here the old trade routes, the railroads, the waterways and the communications lines come together to form a giant nerve center. From here originate the couriers of the Communist Party, the telegrams and telephone calls, the newspapers and broadcasts that direct and guide the whole Soviet empire.

The heart of Moscow is still the Kremlin, whose first stone walls were erected by Grand Duke Dmitri Donskoi in the 14th Century. The massive red brick wall that encloses the medieval fortress one sees today was constructed, however, during the 15th Century reign of Ivan III, who began to build in stone on a large scale, inviting foreign architects and builders, most often Italian, to construct much of the complex of palaces and cathedrals in which Stalin and his successors have entertained leaders from all over the world. It was in the ornate St. George's Hall that Stalin tendered banquets to representatives of the Western world coming to offer help after Hitler's invasion, while German bombers flew overhead and antiaircraft guns mounted in the Kremlin gardens roared, their brilliant muzzle bursts flashing through the red curtains of the palace windows.

Other palaces have been converted into congress halls and Government offices, a museum and a theater. The old churches where once the czars of Russia were crowned, and where many of them lie buried, are now museums through which Soviet tourists reverently shuffle.

The newest building in the Kremlin is the Palace of Congresses. Completed in 1961, during the reign of Nikita Khrushchev, it is a beautifully proportioned modern convention hall of glass and concrete containing restaurants, broad promenades and a theater holding 8,000 people. Despite its modernity, it blends surprisingly well with the traditional Kremlin setting.

JUST outside the walls is "old" Moscow— though few of its houses antedate the great fire of 1812, which swept the city during its brief occupation by Napoleon's troops. Many are one-story palaces designed in the Empire style by architects imported from Italy and France after the Napoleonic Wars. Some are monumental postrevolutionary buildings housing Soviet ministries. In the smaller side streets, huddled below Stalin's seven skyscrapers with their wedding-cake spires, are a number of little wooden houses, the plaster falling from their log walls and their chimneys leaning at precarious angles. These are rapidly disappearing as new apartments rise, and many a Muscovite regrets their passing, as New Yorkers mourn the disappearance of their brownstones.

Farther from the Kremlin and lining the great circular avenues built up in the Stalin era are the new 10- to 15-story apartment buildings, their street façades ornate with balustrades, mosaics and columns, their hidden back walls a drab expanse of raw unplastered brick.

Finally on the outskirts of town where once collective farm cows grazed are the vast, new residential communities built mostly since Stalin's day—massive cubes of unadorned prefabricated cement construction, five to 12 stories high, where individual apartments of two or three rooms are assigned to families on the basis of their need for accommodations.

As Moscow grew to be a great city, so ancient Muscovy grew to be the empire that is the U.S.S.R. today in waves of irresistible expansion followed by long periods of stagnation, foreign invasion and contraction. Among the first and most important of these invasions was that of the Tatars, a Mongolian people who dominated the country for some 250 years, until the end of the 15th Century.

WHILE the rest of Europe was undergoing the great changes of the Middle Ages and the Renaissance, Russia was held fast in the grip of these barbarians. Their highly centralized despotism left its mark on Russian institutions and psychology long after Ivan the Great, the first ruler to use the title of Czar, threw off the Tatar yoke in 1480 and set himself up as "Sovereign of All Russia." Even today Russia's westernmost cities, which managed to escape the rule of the Tatars, retain a more European veneer and a more urbane aspect than their easterly counterparts.

The wave of expansion started by Ivan the Great continued under his son Vasili III and his grandson Ivan the Terrible, who advanced as far as the Baltic in the west, pushed the Tatars behind the Volga in the east and drove the Turks south to the Caspian Sea.

But the wave subsided. "The Time of Troubles"—a period marked by the appearance of a number of claimants to the crown (Russia had four czars in 14 months), foreign intervention, drought, famine and epidemics—followed. Sigismund III of Poland attempted to conquer Russia and in the year 1610 Polish forces occupied Moscow.

The Orthodox Church played a large role in resistance to the invaders, and Moscow was retaken in 1612 by a people's army. With their first aim the election of a czar, a national assembly of nobles, merchants, clergy and soldiers met in 1613 and chose Michael Romanov, a grandnephew of Ivan the Terrible. Michael was the founder of a dynasty that was to rule Russia for more than 300 years, until it was finally deposed by the Revolution of 1917. After another recession in the mid-17th Century, a new surge added the eastern part of the Ukraine, until then an appendage of Poland, with its great, fertile, gently rolling steppes in southwestern Russia.

ONCE again the wave fell back and this time in its wake came the Swedes, who penetrated deep into Russian territory. But in 1709 Peter the Great rallied the country, evicted the invaders from the north and established his frontiers on the shores of the Baltic and the Gulf of Finland. Here on a swamp he had in 1703 begun construction of a new capital, St. Petersburg. Peter's new city was Russia's "Window on Europe." He not only brought Russia out of its own Dark Ages into the stream of European history but he forced Europe upon his reluctant countrymen, introducing Western concepts of administration, industry and warfare. Stripping his nobles of their Oriental robes and clipping their long beards, he even forced them at the point of his dagger to look like Europeans. Half a century later Catherine the Great advanced the western frontiers almost to the point they are today by moving into Poland and Lithuania.

While these great surges brought Russia to the west, other waves of expansion were rolling eastward to the shores of the Pacific, southeastward across the deserts of Central Asia to the foothills of the Himalayas and southward to the borders of Asia Minor.

The first of these eastward advances traveled across the Ural Mountains into Asiatic

Russia, or Siberia. From Moscow's eastern suburbs a ribbon of cleared land nearly 100 yards wide leads eastward across the Volga and over the Urals. This is the great Siberian *Tract*, Russia's centuries-old road to the Pacific.

Although it is asphalted in the vicinity of Moscow and cobblestoned in the neighborhood of provincial cities, the Siberian *Tract* is for the most part a muddy, unpaved trail. As you follow it to the east you are treading in the footsteps of tens of thousands of exiles who since the 17th Century have stumbled along it to work the mines and forests of Siberia. Here and there are still visible the *etapes,* or stations, where the exiles and convicts camped overnight on their way to oblivion.

As it climbs the gentle, wooded western slopes of the Ural Mountains the *Tract* leads past a cement obelisk that marks the dividing line between Asia and Europe. A few miles farther the *Tract* comes to Sverdlovsk, formerly Ekaterinburg, on the eastern slopes of the mountains. Here in 1918 Nicholas II, the last of the czars, was executed with his family by Bolshevik guards.

Sverdlovsk also boasts one of the world's greatest geological museums, a magnificent display case for the mineral wealth of the Ural area. As early as the 18th Century the Ural mines had attracted the attention of Russia's rulers, who thereupon looked for labor to exploit them. In 1753 capital punishment had been abolished in Russia and in its place perpetual exile in Siberia was substituted. But then with the need for labor the list of offenses punishable by Siberian exile steadily expanded, and from year to year the dreary columns of prisoners trudging along the great Siberian *Tract* grew larger and larger.

LONG after the czarist regime had disappeared the exile system was continued and expanded. While under the czars undesirables frequently were forced merely to reside in Siberia and even received pensions during their banishment, Stalin reduced their status virtually to that of slaves. Under him several million persons are thought to have been sentenced to exile and forced to work not only the mines and the forests but other projects being built to provide a second industrial base behind the Urals. Many who survived their sentences were compelled to settle on the inhospitable land. Later Stalin's successor Nikita Khrushchev recognized that forced labor is unprofitable and eliminated the worst iniquities of the system. In the place of convicts the Kremlin sought to recruit young settlers by the lure of high wages and special bonuses to work the mines, the power projects and the factories being built in this remote area.

Beyond Sverdlovsk the *Tract* sweeps through great forests that hold the bulk of Russia's lumber reserves. The opening of the Trans-Siberian Railroad in the late 19th Century made it possible to move the raw timber to western markets. But until then Siberia had suffered from an almost fatal economic deficiency—a lack of effective transportation.

BETWEEN the Urals and the Pacific, Siberia is cut by a number of major rivers. But all of them flow north through virgin forests into the frozen tundra and thence to the Arctic Ocean, which until recently was icebound a large part of the year. The railroad solved the problem of extracting the lumber. Large-scale development of western Siberia began in 1930. And today the rivers are being exploited for hydroelectric power. The Bratsk hydroelectric plant, finished in 1961, ultimately will be able to generate 4.5 million kilowatts, more than twice the power of the Grand Coulee project in the United States. An even larger plant is under construction near Krasnoyarsk on the Yenisei River, and the site has been surveyed for still a third at Ust-Ilim, 200 miles north of Bratsk.

Until recently the area north of the Trans-Siberian Railroad was scarcely inhabited outside of the camps of slave labor working the forests, the salt mines north of Irkutsk and the gold fields of the Lena River. During a day's journey down one of the major rivers one could

13

expect to pass perhaps a single fishermen's village, its log cabins clinging to the banks of the swift, muddy, log-infested river.

Here only bear, lynx, sable and beaver provided oldtime trappers with a livelihood. But today entire communities of new, modern homes have grown up to house the workers in the factories that are being built to utilize the new hydroelectric power.

SOUTH of the Siberian *Tract* and the Trans-Siberian Railroad are the beginnings of the Central Asian deserts: the dry plains of Kazakhstan where until a generation ago Mongol-featured nomads camped in their black tents and grazed their sheep on the sparse desert grasses. This is a bleak-looking country, treeless and seemingly waterless, though beneath the soil Soviet scientists have recently discovered gigantic underground lakes. In summer only the desert grasses hold the parched soil in place against 60-mile-an-hour winds. In winter the gales raise snowdrifts 50 feet high.

Starting in 1954 thousands of Communist youth workers were sent by the Kremlin to the Kazakhstan plains to plow the soil and plant wheat to supplement the Soviet Union's chronically short food supply. Today the giant state farms they built—wooden barns, barracks, sheds, schools and stores—occasionally break the monotony of the flat, sun-baked landscape.

The Siberian *Tract* ends at Irkutsk, but the Trans-Siberian Railroad continues. Presently it comes to Lake Baikal, the deepest inland body of water in the world. Then it plunges on through the forests of larch and pine to the Amur River, which marks the border of Manchuria, and thence along the Amur in a giant bow to Vladivostok on the Pacific, 4,000 miles from Moscow.

While Catherine the Great's diplomats were pushing Poland's frontiers toward the west and freebooters were cutting their way across the Siberian wilderness, another great wave of Russian expansion headed southward across the Caucasus. As early as the reign of Ivan the Terrible, Cossack troops—mercenaries drawn

primarily from the Ukraine—had reached the mouth of the Volga on the Caspian Sea. Today Astrakhan, where they established a settlement, is a major fishing center and a main source of the world's caviar.

Peter the Great tried to push the frontier farther south to Baku, then a part of Persia, but without success. Not until 1813 did Russia obtain possession of Baku (one of the Soviet Union's principal oil sources). In 1828 the frontier was placed at the Araks River, which flows into the Caspian near its southern end. Here the border has remained until this day despite efforts by Stalin to push it southward after World War II.

WEST of Baku and bounded by mountains to the north and south lie the fertile, semitropical valleys of Georgia. They are famous for their wines and their fierce men, a leading example of whom was Joseph Stalin, the shoemaker's son and onetime seminary student who clawed his way to the top of the Russian Communist Party and ruthlessly ruled the Soviet Union until his death in 1953.

Two centuries ago Georgia was a tiny Christian kingdom surrounded by hostile Moslem states and tribes. In the late 18th Century it was granted status as a protectorate of Russia and was annexed in 1801 when Georgia's last king abdicated in favor of the czar.

Between Russia proper and Tbilisi, the cosmopolitan, almost Western capital of Georgia, lie the rugged and spectacularly beautiful Caucasus Mountains stretching from the Caspian to the Black Sea and reaching snow-clad peaks as high as 18,500 feet.

The high mountain valleys are inhabited by fierce mountain tribes, including the Chechen, Ingush and Kabardin who for centuries resisted every attempt of the Russians to pacify them or interfere with their independent tribal life. In an effort to subdue their resistance and to improve access to Georgia the Imperial Government began in 1814 to build the Georgian Military Road joining Tbilisi with the north. Even today, despite modern snowplows, this spectacular road, which clings to precipitous mountainsides and winds over high passes, is often closed by ice and snow for several months each year.

The highway did provide access but it did not enable imperial troops to overcome the resistance of the tribes. Even after the Revolution, isolated in their valleys, they continued to resist attempts to "communize" them until the Second World War. Then, when the Germans approached, they put themselves at the disposal of the invader against their historic foes, the Russians. But when the Nazis were finally pushed back Stalin took his revenge. In one day hundreds of thousands of the mountain people were rounded up, herded into cattle cars and shipped off to the plains of Kazakhstan. Not until the dictator was dead were the survivors allowed to return to their mountain home—defeated and dispirited relics of their ancient tradition.

The last of the extensive waves of Russian expansion prior to World War II was directed southeast into Central Asia. Though the czars, particularly Peter the Great, had long dreamed of an overland route to India, the long desert belt called the Hungry Steppe, which separates Central Asia from Russia, discouraged him and his successors.

Not until 1865 did a Russian expeditionary force under the command of General Konstantin Kaufmann capture the Moslem town of Tashkent. It soon became the military headquarters from which further expeditions were sent to subdue the emirates of Samarkand, Bukhara, Khiva and Kokand. By 1883 the most remote of all the principalities, Mary, was captured and the borders of the Russian empire were extended to the frontier of Afghanistan, where they have since remained.

### PEOPLES OF THE SOVIET UNION

Below are figures from the 1959 Soviet census. The population today is estimated to be 229.1 million.

| | |
|---|---|
| Russians | 114,113,579 |
| Ukrainians | 37,252,930 |
| Byelorussians | 7,913,488 |
| Uzbeks | 6,015,416 |
| Tatars | 4,967,701 |
| Kazakhs | 3,621,610 |
| Azerbaidzhanians | 2,939,728 |
| Armenians | 2,786,912 |
| Georgians | 2,691,950 |
| Lithuanians | 2,326,094 |
| Jews | 2,267,814 |
| Moldavians | 2,214,139 |
| Others | 19,715,289 |
| Total | 208,826,650 |

Tashkent, the leading city and transportation center of the area, is one of the fast-developing cities in Russia. With a population of more than one million, it has a neat, modern airport, long, broad canals, and rich surrounding land studded with orchards and vineyards. It has perhaps more foreign students than Moscow.

Tashkent is really three separate cities: an old native quarter in which flat-roofed, white-washed houses cluster together along narrow lanes; a European quarter dating from the first Russian occupation and containing wide, shady streets and open squares bordered with one- and two-story bungalows of Victorian design; and the New City, built under Soviet rule. In the latter an ornate opera house faces on an enormous square typical of the Stalin period of city planning.

The square is a favorite spot for Tashkenters to sit while enjoying the cooling breezes from the water of a tremendous fountain whose spouts send up jets of water 20 and 30 feet into the air. Across the square stands the city's large, imposing hotel, a gleaming white structure which is elaborately adorned with Persian arches and alabaster filigree.

At one corner of the hotel is an outdoor "shashlik" restaurant where the smell of mutton roasting on a charcoal grill reminds you that you are in the very heart of Central Asia. Around the tables sit Uzbeks, small, wiry men, their Eastern faces brown and wrinkled, wisps of beards dangling from their chins, their short-cropped heads covered with black-and-white skullcaps. Some of the women still wear the *khalat*, or dress, of rich red-and-yellow stripes. Even younger women retain the traditional hair style of long braids.

Not far from the main square is a shopping quarter built chiefly before the Revolution. Here

15

Uzbeks, Kazakhs and Tadzhiks from the outlying towns and villages come to buy the small luxuries that their provincial shops do not carry: ready-made suits, dresses and, above all, shoes. The visitor must push and elbow his way through excited but good-natured crowds to get to the counter to buy himself the straw hat that he will certainly need to protect himself against the glaring Central Asian sun.

Tashkent lies in the center of a well-watered oasis where small farms once produced wheat and melons. Today the fields are consolidated into giant farms that supply the Soviet Union with more than half of its cotton.

Roughly 180 miles southwest of Tashkent is the ancient capital of all Central Asia, Samarkand, one of the oldest cities in the world. Like every Eastern city from Morocco to Indonesia, Samarkand has its bazaar where traders and farmers sit cross-legged in their booths, surrounded by their wares: round, flat disks of unleavened bread, a dozen varieties of melons, jars of saffron, curry powder and a dozen more herbs whose pungent smells fill the air.

Samarkand also has a modern shopping street where state-owned stores sell perfume from Moscow, shoes from Czechoslovakia and toys from East Germany. But even for Soviet officials Samarkand's greatest boasts are the Moslem seminaries and mosques of the ancient civilization of Tamerlane, who himself lies buried in a beautiful blue-tiled tomb in the heart of the town.

WHAT kinds of people occupy this sprawling empire? Few generalizations can apply to a conglomeration of peoples who speak a hundred languages and dialects and whose racial and cultural origins spring from a score of civilizations from ancient Greece to Genghis Khan's Mongolia. What can the Moscow intellectual whose forefathers debated with Goethe and Voltaire have in common with a prime minister of Kazakhstan who was born in a nomad camp the son of a Mongolian sheepherder?

Despite this intermingling of peoples, the Russians continue to dominate the country.

The republics, it is true, have been producing more of the new bureaucrats, and in Tbilisi, Tashkent and Alma Ata the figureheads of local government may be Georgians, Uzbeks or Kazakhs, but the party bosses behind the scenes most frequently are descendants of the colonizers and conquerors. They are Russians and, on occasion, Ukrainians.

Essentially the inhabitants of the U.S.S.R. are a relatively unsophisticated people in the sense that they have not yet been sophisticated by cosmopolitan life, softened by modern comforts or confused by the plethora of choices that are available in a highly developed community. Like their land, their thoughts and ideas are large, plain and open.

BEHIND their hard exteriors one can detect in the peoples of Russia traces of their turbulent history: the fatalism inherited from their traditional Orthodox religion, the suspicion and fear of foreigners that derives from their acute awareness of the vulnerability of their frontiers.

Toward those who have aroused their ire the Russians can be implacable, as anyone can attest who has seen them marching into action against an enemy—endless solid ranks doggedly advancing. The whine of dive bombers, the crash of artillery and the chatter of machine guns may have told them that directly ahead lies a narrow defile or perhaps a tottering bridge that they must pass if they are to survive. Below their low-slung helmets their faces are almost inhumanly stolid and from deep in their throats comes a low, defiant, almost religious battle song promising death to their enemies and victory for their fatherland.

But left alone the Russians can be a friendly people. Cut off through much of their history from the outside world, they are intensely curious about life beyond their national horizons, and when their fears and suspicions are allayed they are both amicable and hospitable to visitors, and especially to Americans, anxious to impress the visitors with present accomplishments and future plans.

*Shrouded in the winter haze, the Byzantine domes of St. Andrew's Church overlook the city of Kiev, Russia's capital centuries ago.*

# Vast and Varied Domain

The Russia of fact—as well as of legend—is a country of such grandiose scale and remoteness that it seems to dwarf man. Stretching from the Baltic and Black Seas to the Pacific Ocean, from the Arctic Ocean to the borders of China, Mongolia and the Middle Eastern nations, the U.S.S.R. covers more than a seventh of the earth's surface, making it the world's largest single state. The consolidation of such a vast and disparate land is one of the great achievements of the 20th Century—and its modernization is one of the great challenges that now face the Russian people.

17

IN GORKY on the Volga River, two children visit the city's ancient showpiece, a tall 14th Century "kremlin," or fortress, whose wall and tower dominate the river port.

EUROPEAN RUSSIA *has a strong visual and cultural affinity with the West. Its people, mostly Slavic, dominate the rest of the U.S.S.R.*

**ALONG THE VOLGA**, the main artery of western Russia, a two-way traffic of barges moves at sunset.

**IN THE UKRAINE**, breadbasket of the U.S.S.R., a lone teamster drives out to collect firewood.

19

## A CAPITAL TRANSFORMED *by winter's magic,*
*Moscow in the snow becomes a city of cold, strange beauty*

**FESTIVE TROIKAS**, bright with color, glide along a snowy road on the city's outskirts, heading for the sport in Izmailovsky Park.

**GLOOMY RED SQUARE** is touched by the wan glow of a low morning sun. Street lights are kept on to cheer the work-bound.

# MOUNTAINOUS GEORGIA, *long a wild land that sheltered fierce men, is being tamed*

**NEW MACHINES,** combines that can pick up to two tons of tea a day, replace hand labor on a Georgian collective (*above*). A good laborer used to pick 50 or 60 pounds.

**RUGGED PASSES,** with tilled fields on their slopes (*right*), helped Georgians repel invaders. A few horsemen, like the rider on the river bed (*bottom*), could hold off an army.

**IN THE KIRGIZ RANGE** in Soviet Central Asia a shepherd drives his sheep up from their wintering on a lower slope. The sheep are the property of the Soviet state. The people of Soviet Central Asia, while stubbornly individualistic by tradition, have profited greatly in recent years from modern farming methods introduced by the state.

SOVIET CENTRAL ASIA, *largely a cotton-growing area, has been predominantly Islamic for centuries. There are some 30 million Moslems and former Moslems in the Soviet Union*

**CARAVAN OF HAY** makes its way across the steppe near Bukhara, former capital of the ancient emirate of Bukhara and long a center of Islamic culture.

**AGED DRIVER** of a heavily laden wagon plods along between Alma-Ata, capital of the Kazakh Republic, and Frunze, capital of the Kirgiz Republic.

25

# THE NEW SIBERIA, *no longer considered a wasteland, contributes to the growing Soviet economy*

CITY CORNER in Khabarovsk (*above*), a hub of the continent-spanning Trans-Siberian Railroad, sports a European-style pillar for notices. The city is located in the far eastern part of the Soviet Union on the Chinese border.

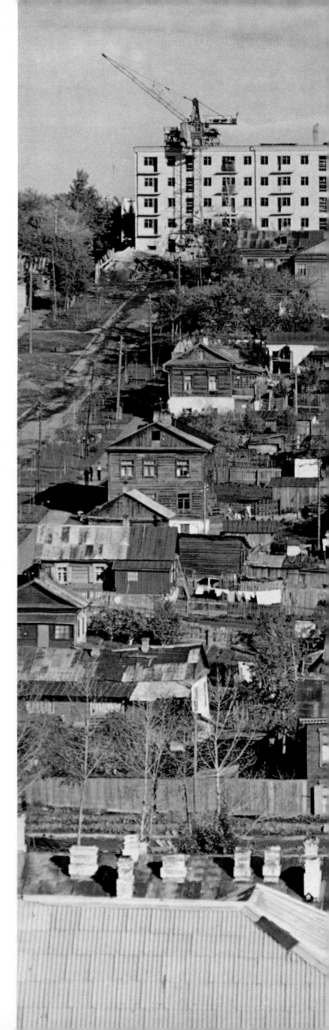

OLD ROAD made from logs is repaired by Siberian men and women who fit sawed sections of timber together (*above*). The new sections last only eight years because of the permanently frozen ground on which they are laid.

NEW APARTMENTS rise above the old wooden houses of Khabarovsk (*left*). The Government is determined to develop its eastern Siberian frontier, and new construction is altering the traditional image of a barren Siberia.

CRUCIAL MOMENT of the Revolution came when Lenin returned from exile. He masterminded the Bolshevik victory over groups that had forced the Czar's abdication.

# The Rise of the Communist State

THE drive that over the years pushed Russia's frontiers constantly outward was until 50 years ago the product of three basic forces: the restlessness of Russia's rugged population, the rulers' fear of being crushed by their neighbors, and plain human covetousness. Perhaps, too, the drive was spurred by the curiosity that impels the inhabitants of a rolling plain to push on to the top of the next rise just to see what is on the other side. But in this century a dynamic new element was added to these age-old compulsions, making Russian expansionism a challenge not just to its neighbors but to the entire globe. That element was international Communism.

The father of Communism, Karl Marx, once predicted that countries more advanced industrially than Russia would be earlier in adopting the cure he so fanatically recommended for the world's ills. As in so many of his other predictions he turned out to be wrong. Why? The answer is perhaps a dual one: the peculiarly distressing ills caused by Czarism, and a man named Lenin.

The cruel autocratic rule of the czars was a heritage partly of the Mongol khans and partly of the Byzantine Empire that had flourished to the south. For centuries that rule was personified by tyrannical landlords, corrupt tax collectors, brutal conscription officers, bigoted Orthodox priests and finally the monstrous bureaucracy that enforced the laws tying the peasants to the soil as serfs or virtual slaves.

As early as 1773, during the reign of Catherine the Great, a widespread revolt broke out under the leadership of a Cossack named Emelyan Pugachev. Its chief grievances were the harsh rules of military service, the injustices of serfdom and the Church's suppression of religious freedom. The revolt was suppressed but the grievances remained and continued through the first half of the 19th Century to stir up outbursts of peasant violence.

In December 1825 a small group of reformers, inspired by Western experiments in constitutional government, attempted to stage an uprising. But this, too, was suppressed.

With the tension mounting, Alexander II, a Czar with more realistic views than his predecessors, came to the imperial throne in 1855. Acknowledging the necessity for reform, he took the first major step by liberating the serfs. But other desperately needed reforms were slow in coming. After Alexander was assassinated in 1881 another wave of reaction set in.

But unrest was steadily growing in the countryside. Organized bands of peasants raided the mansions of local landlords, burning their records, confiscating their grain and carrying off their farm implements.

In St. Petersburg and Moscow a growing army of workers, attracted from the farms by the first surge of Russian industrialization, was stirring restlessly. The first big break came in 1905. An extraordinarily able priest, Father Georgi Gapon, had organized a society of industrial workers in St. Petersburg. Gapon advocated reform through mass appeal to the Czar himself, Nicholas II. On a January Sunday, Gapon's followers formed a procession and marched to the Winter Palace, singing "God Save the Czar," to present a peaceful petition for relief.

A panicky officer ordered the Czar's troops to fire, and a sheet of bullets poured into the solid mass of humans. Hundreds were mowed down, their portraits of the Czar and crosses falling with them. "Bloody Sunday" was the last organized attempt to win reforms by appeal.

In the autumn of that year factory workers staged a general strike in St. Petersburg and organized themselves into a *soviet*, or council. This was the high point of the "1905 Revolution," and it so frightened Nicholas that he acceded to the formation of a legislative body by election. But the Duma, as the resulting parliament was called, was strictly limited in power and dominated by a restricted electorate. While moderate political parties continued to operate in the open, the more revolutionary organizations flourished underground. Finally the reverses of the First World War ignited the substructure and set the entire ramshackle system in flames.

The immediate causes of the conflagration were readily apparent. Both the Army and the home front were disillusioned by defeats; severe economic shortages were gripping the hinterland; the cumbersome czarist bureaucracy was hopelessly unable to cope with its problems; and finally there were scandals in the imperial palace itself, centering around a dissolute, self-appointed peasant "healer," Grigori Rasputin.

Discontent among workers, soldiers, generals and politicians reached the breaking point in February (March by the Western calendar) of 1917. Organizing themselves into a *soviet*, the workers of Petrograd (as St. Petersburg had been renamed during the war) were shouting for reform. In a few days they were joined by soldiers. In the Duma political leaders agitated for the formation of a responsible Cabinet to end the constant chaos.

Nicholas II, a kindly but stupid man imbued with his absolute autocracy, had up to now ignored all warnings. When the Duma President, Mikhail Rodzianko, sent him a plea for concessions, Nicholas commented: "This fat Rodzianko has written me some nonsense to which I will not even reply." Instead he ordered the Duma dispersed.

BUT the Duma refused and with the approval of delegates from the Petrograd Council of Workers' and Soldiers' Deputies (called the Petrograd Soviet for short) it formed a provisional Government and promised a constituent assembly to draft the long-sought constitution. The Czar ordered his troops to suppress the revolutionary Government, but the generals were already pledging their support to it. On March 15 Nicholas abdicated.

The provisional Government ushered in by the so-called February Revolution was a moderate one and included representatives of the Duma and the Petrograd Soviet. It was headed by a somewhat colorless liberal, Prince Georgi Lvov, and its chief link with the more radical Soviet was Aleksandr Kerenski, by far the most energetic member of the Cabinet.

The provisional Government soon found itself facing incredibly difficult problems. At the military front resistance was dwindling. Behind the front there were severe shortages. The manufacture of war supplies had dropped off, and there was unrest among peasants and workers.

But at this point another factor emerged. It was destined to transform the entire Revolution. Its roots had been planted some 70 years earlier when the brilliant and bitter German economist and revolutionary Karl Marx proclaimed Communism the key to the future. Burrowing in the archives of the British Museum in London, he had evolved an elaborate "scientific" justification of the inevitability of Communism to be achieved through class struggle. While he based his views on the glaring injustices of the early industrialization through which Britain was then passing, he claimed a universal application of his theory and program.

Marx's system envisaged the abolition of private ownership by violent proletarian revolution, the gradual withering away of national states and a universal order based on a simple principle: "From each according to his abilities; to each according to his needs." This system, Marx insisted, would displace capitalism everywhere and spread throughout the world.

Marx's *Communist Manifesto*, proclaiming the inevitable doom of capitalism, had been published in 1848. In the next generation it had won many disciples throughout Europe, among them a group of Russian revolutionaries who in 1898 had formed the Russian Social Democratic Party.

AMONG its adherents was a provincial Russian intellectual, Vladimir Ilyich Ulyanov, who used the pseudonym Lenin or N. Lenin. A short, nervous, intensely single-minded man and an ardent Marxist, Lenin was, above all, a genius in the field of political maneuver. Disgusted with the "go slow" tactics of moderate revolutionaries, he insisted that his party become a tightly organized band.

"Lenin," wrote Maxim Gorki, the revolutionary writer, "was a man who prevented people from leading their accustomed lives as no one before him was able to do." His insistence on selfless discipline, the keystone to his eventual success, was resisted among Social Democrats. In 1903 the party split. One part, the alleged majority, or "Bolsheviks" (the word comes from the term for "majority," though actually they were a minority), sided with Lenin. The "Mensheviks," or minority, rejected his demands for a totalitarian party.

Lenin, after being twice banished to Siberia for revolutionary activities, had left Russia in 1900 and continued his efforts to organize the revolution from abroad. He returned during the 1905 Revolution, left again two years later and lived in Switzerland during the First World War. It was there that he learned of the February Revolution and from there that he arranged with the German Government—which suspected that his presence in Petrograd might accelerate popular agitation against the war—to cross Germany into Sweden.

Once in Petrograd, Lenin rallied the Bolsheviks, who had been vacillating between cooperating with the provisional Government and fighting it. Stepping up the party's propaganda activities and agitation among the Petrograd troops, he maneuvered to get his men in control of the Petrograd Soviet. "All power to the Soviets!" was the slogan he proclaimed.

BUT an abortive Bolshevik uprising in July, sparked by the collapse of the Russian war offensive, forced Lenin to flee again, this time to Finland, where he continued to urge the seizure of power by the Bolsheviks. Convinced by his driving energy and self-assurance, the Bolsheviks redoubled their efforts to win over the troops in Petrograd. In September they gained control of the Petrograd Soviet and in October elected Leon Trotsky, Lenin's ablest and chief aide, as its president.

Lenin returned to Russia on October 23, determined to strike against the Government on the opening of the All-Russian Congress of the Soviets on October 25 (November 7 by the Western calendar). "October twenty-fourth was too early," he told his uncertain followers. "October twenty-sixth will be too late." He ordered his Bolshevik bands and Army supporters to take over all Government buildings, including the Winter Palace, where Kerenski, the head of the Government since Lvov's resignation in July, and his Cabinet were trying desperately to rally loyal troops.

Faced by mounting mutiny, Kerenski at 10 a.m. slipped out of the city in an American Embassy car draped with an American flag, hoping to rally troops at the front to march on the capital and throw out the Bolsheviks. But even the high command was deaf to his pleas. Before he could return to the capital Petrograd had fallen into Lenin's hands. Within a few days the disciplined Communist conspirators posted in Russia's principal cities took over the local governments. Kerenski escaped to Paris, and

eventually to the U.S. The October Revolution, to the amazement of the world—including many Communists—was an accomplished fact.

A dictatorship of the proletariat was set up by the organization of the Council of People's Commissars, with Lenin as Chairman and Trotsky as Minister of Foreign Affairs. Their first official act was to issue a Decree of Peace calling for an armistice among the warring nations with "no annexation, no indemnities." Almost immediately they followed that with a decree authorizing village committees to seize private lands and distribute them to the peasants.

The Allies turned down the peace decree, but the Germans agreed to negotiate and some weeks later Trotsky led a peace delegation to Brest-Litovsk. From the Russian train pamphlets were scattered calling upon German troops to revolt. All during the negotiations that led to a peace treaty in 1918 it was obvious that Trotsky was playing for time for the pamphlets to take effect and to spark the revolution he hoped for in Germany.

ON the very first day after the Revolution Trotsky had declaimed: "Either the Russian revolution will raise the whirlwind of struggle in the west, or the capitalists of all countries will crush our revolution. . . ."

Trotsky was wrong on both counts. But in the three-year civil war that followed the Revolution the European powers did come within an ace of defeating the Bolsheviks' Red Army, which had been hastily organized by Trotsky. Anti-Bolshevik, or "White Russian," troops attacked from every quarter, and in the course of the war American, British, French, German, Serbian, Polish and Japanese forces intervened in support of the Whites. In May 1918 the Czech Legion, a 40,000-man group made up partly of men from Czech colonies in the former Russian empire and partly of defectors from the Austro-Hungarian Army, turned on the Bolsheviks. The Legion, which had been withdrawing to Vladivostok through Siberia, launched an offensive westward and was successful in capturing several strategic centers.

As it came closer to Ekaterinburg, where the former Czar and his family were being held, Lenin evidently feared that Nicholas would be rescued and become the focal point of a counterrevolutionary movement. He ordered the execution of the royal family.

ALL the attacks, including the Legion's, were repulsed, but not until the revived Polish state, which had attacked in the west, had been turned back were the last White armies driven from Russian soil. By the end of 1920 the Communists were masters of Russia.

Four factors prevented the defeat of what was originally a pitifully weak Bolshevik Government: the divided leadership of the White Russian troops; the failure of the White Russians to arouse popular backing; growing Russian suspicion of all foreign intervention; and finally the Red Army's strategic position at the core of the country's transportation network.

Even while the White and foreign troops were trying to upset the Soviet regime, the Communists were hopeful that the proletarian uprising so confidently predicted by Lenin and Trotsky would somehow take place in Western Europe. In 1919 the Communist International, or Comintern, was organized to assist these hoped-for revolutions. A revolt did occur in 1919 in Berlin, and Communist regimes held power for brief periods in Bavaria, Hungary and other areas. But as the new governments of Western and Central Europe regained stability Communist uprisings ceased.

Indeed a new kind of revolt now occurred. In March 1921 sailors at Kronshtadt, a naval base guarding the Petrograd harbor, struck briefly against the Communist rule. Concurrently there were peasant uprisings.

These revolts were symptoms of the disorganization and discontent that had engulfed Russia. Six and a half years of war, revolution and foreign intervention had left the country starving, its factories scarcely operating, its peasants refusing to part with their food to feed the cities. In 1921 a severe famine caused great loss of life in several rich agricultural areas. Lenin was forced into a major economic retreat.

Embarking that year on a New Economic Policy (called NEP), the Communist government relaxed its earlier measures to establish Communism and permitted the re-establishment of private trade and small-scale private industry. The economy rapidly revived.

Abroad, too, the Communists faced setbacks. The much-awaited world revolution had failed to materialize. Here again Lenin called for a retreat and instructed the Communist parties abroad to cooperate with other Left-Wing parties. Instead of trying to overthrow governments, they were to enter the ranks of trade unions so as to establish their leadership of the working class. The ultimate purpose was to use this leadership to foment revolution.

In 1922 Lenin suffered a stroke and a relatively unknown party leader, a gruff and wily Georgian called Joseph Stalin, began a campaign to oust Trotsky as second-in-command and heir presumptive to Lenin. Many issues separated Stalin and Trotsky, although both men aimed at world revolution and the building of socialism in Russia. But while Trotsky maintained that without world revolution socialism in the Soviet Union was doomed, Stalin believed that if socialism were firmly established in Russia, Communist planning for all other countries could be centralized.

STALIN won the fight in the years after Lenin's death in 1924 partly because he was shrewder and more ruthless than Trotsky. But his program also implied greater confidence in Russia's strength, which made him—and it—more popular with the party membership.

In the end Trotsky was expelled from the party, banished from Russia and finally murdered in Mexico in 1940. From 1927 until his own death in 1953 Stalin was the undisputed dictator of the Soviet Union.

By proclaiming his intention of building socialism in one country, Stalin did not mean to abandon the Communist dream of world revolution. It was rather a question of emphasis:

the industrialization of Russia came first; attempts to stir revolution came second.

Forced by the necessity of securing foreign credits and luring Western technicians to assist his industrialization drive, beset by peasant resistance to his agricultural reforms and obsessed by fears of opposition from Old Bolsheviks, Stalin consistently subordinated his interest in Communist parties abroad to his immediate aim of strengthening Russia.

PERHAPS his greatest mistake in the early 1930s was made just as Hitler was making his bid for power. Rather than permit a Left-Wing, anti-Communist government in Germany, Stalin ordered the German Communists to side with the reactionary Nazis against the moderate Left, thus giving Hitler a considerable boost in his rise to power.

In 1934, alarmed now by Hitler's anti-Russian pronouncements, Russia joined the League of Nations. The following year it concluded an alliance with France and with Czechoslovakia. The Franco-Soviet pact was a factor in Hitler's decision to seize the Rhineland in 1936.

The outbreak of the Spanish Civil War that same year presented Stalin with a dilemma. On the one hand, the existence of Fascist regimes in Italy and Germany held a threat, for a Fascist victory in Spain might help bring about a Rightist coalition against him in Europe. Yet military aid involved sending Soviet personnel through other countries where more idealistic revolutionaries might "contaminate" them. Stalin vacillated. At first he permitted all-out military intervention with Soviet technicians and advisers and Communist-recruited international brigades. Then, changing course, he ordered his officers home.

When the Western powers at Munich in 1938 gave the Sudetenland to Germany without consulting Russia, they effectively drove Stalin into Hitler's arms. In 1939 negotiations for an alliance between Russia, France and Britain came to naught and in August of that year Stalin surprised the world by signing a nonaggression pact with Hitler. The two dictators agreed to split Poland and the rest of Eastern Europe between them, thereby assuring Hitler peace on the eastern frontier in the event that France and Britain went to war over Poland.

That this involved a sudden and radical switch of policy for the Western Communist parties did not disturb Stalin. His sole aim was to gain time to create an industrial base in Russia with which he might defend "the citadel of Communism."

But then on the warm Sunday morning of June 22, 1941, early strollers in Moscow's streets were startled by a voice over the loudspeakers mounted at every corner: "Attention! Citizens! Shortly you will hear an important Government announcement." After a few hours they heard the shaky voice of Foreign Minister Vyacheslav Molotov telling them of the attack launched against them by Germany.

Twelve days later Stalin himself went on the air. In his harsh, guttural accent he appealed to his people to resist, in the name not of Communism but of country. This was no ideological war, where the sympathies of his people might be divided. This was a patriotic war to defend Russian soil.

The events of Hitler's invasion are still remembered by most Americans. There was the initial German advance to the gates of Moscow, the second Nazi surge to the Volga and the resistance at Stalingrad. Finally the tide turned and the Russian armies advanced slowly and relentlessly to Berlin and Vienna, ultimately meeting the Western Allies on the Elbe River.

WITHIN a month of the 1941 Hitler attack Britain and the U.S., recognizing that Nazi Germany was the most imminent menace, had pledged their support to the Russian forces, and during the course of hostilities they had shipped 12 billion dollars' worth of munitions, equipment and food to the Soviet Union. Yet they still feared a Communist worldwide movement and so sought to reach agreement with Stalin on a postwar world order.

At Allied meetings in Tehran, Yalta and Potsdam, Stalin pledged himself to a policy of continued cooperation after the war. Specifically he agreed to popular election of governments in the areas overrun by Soviet troops and to a joint administration of occupied Germany. In the Far East he agreed to support Chiang Kai-shek's Chinese Government in defeating the Japanese, but only in return for a special position in Manchuria.

AS the war came to an end, however, the Soviet Government repudiated each of these agreements in turn. In Poland, Hungary, Romania and Bulgaria regimes were established whose key posts were manned by Communists trained in Moscow. In Germany the four-power occupation disintegrated into two occupations, one in the west by the U.S., Britain and France and another in the east by Russia.

What motivated Stalin to cast aside all these agreements when his country lay devastated, its population exhausted by the war? Many Western statesmen had believed that at least in the immediate postwar years Stalin would cultivate his alliances with the West as a source of loans, supplies and aid in rehabilitating his country. In this belief they had put their faith in the Tehran, Yalta and Potsdam agreements. But the war had hardly ended when Stalin again proclaimed his revolutionary goal and decided to go it alone. He strained his relations with the West to the very brink of war at a time when the United States alone had the secret of the atomic bomb.

In part Stalin's aggressive drive can be attributed to that fundamental tenet of Marxian belief, world revolution. But Stalin's motivation went further. The Russian people's acute awareness of the vulnerability of their frontiers had been newly aroused by the German attack, and it had been enhanced by a deep patriotism caused by their survival. Stalin was therefore impelled to make every effort to secure Russia's frontiers once and for all.

To this end, and despite his promises, Stalin insisted on establishing a ring of Communist satellite nations in the west. His attempt to take over Greece with Moscow-supported guerrilla

forces was blocked only by U.S. support of the anti-Communist forces.

In France and Italy, Stalin tried to exploit postwar economic dislocations so as to bring about popular dissatisfaction as a prelude to the establishment of Communist governments, but the attempt was forestalled by Marshall Plan economic aid from the U.S., which provided the initial stability that these Governments needed.

In 1948 pro-Soviet groups in Czechoslovakia, once a bastion of democracy in Eastern Europe, organized a coup that put Communists in undisputed control. That same year Stalin attempted to take over West Berlin by blockading Allied troops in the city. He was thwarted by a Western airlift, and eventually he lifted the blockade.

Only in one area was Stalin forced to retreat from the position he held in Europe when the war ended. That was Yugoslavia. There the Communist regime led by Josip Broz Tito, which had established itself during the war with little assistance from Moscow, was for a time Stalin's staunchest ally in Eastern Europe. But Stalin's attempt to seize control of the Yugoslav Army, secret police and party apparatus so alienated Tito that Stalin was forced to break with him in 1948.

IN the Far East a different pattern developed. In China itself Stalin had what appeared to the world as his most spectacular and, to him, his most unexpected success. With relatively little Soviet aid the Chinese Communists succeeded in ousting the corrupt Chiang Kai-shek regime from the Chinese mainland and took control of China.

In 1950 Stalin attempted his most daring thrust, an attack into South Korea, using troops from pro-Soviet North Korea. But South Korean and American troops, assisted by other United Nations forces, succeeded in forcing back the attackers and their Chinese allies. In Malaya, Burma, Indonesia and the Philippines, Stalin incited Communist rebellions, but all were suppressed. He was more successful in

Vietnam, where Communist-led Vietminh troops assisted by the Chinese Communists were able to win a partition of the country.

When Stalin died in 1953, his frightened successors realized that until they had established authority over their subjects they must avoid all risks abroad and challenges at home by relaxing the intolerable Stalinist system of rule by terror. But Stalin was hardly buried when friction developed between them and the Chinese, who apparently resented their assumption of leadership over the Communist movement. Though Moscow continued to furnish economic aid to Peking for a time and though the differences between the two capitals were slow to appear in public, eventually the rivalry between the two Communist centers exploded into the open. The Chinese Communists, having established themselves largely by their own efforts (as Tito had done), were fired with a fanaticism reminiscent of that which had prevailed in Russia in the 1920s. Militant, ambitious, fervent in their faith in the ultimate world victory of Communism, they scorned what they considered the timid tactics of Stalin's successors, who, faced with American nuclear might, were fearful of losing the industrial giant that they had produced.

Rejecting Moscow's leadership, Peking prodded its protégés in North Vietnam to step up their guerrilla attacks on U.S.-supported South Vietnam. Throughout the world, particularly in Africa and Latin America, the Chinese vied openly with Moscow-oriented Communist parties for leadership of the radical Left.

IN Europe, meantime, the results of the post-Stalin relaxation were dramatic and even tragic. Almost at once discontented East Germany erupted in demonstrations that had to be put down by Soviet tanks. Unrest in Poland grew until in 1956 an upsurge of nationalist feeling, which was shared even by Communists, broke into open rebellion against Moscow and the Stalin-appointed regime. This resulted in the restoration to power of Wladyslaw Gomulka, a nationalist Communist leader whom Stalin had jailed. Thereafter the Warsaw Government steered a steady, cautious course out from under Moscow domination.

In Hungary a more violent outbreak followed the Polish uprising, and civil war raged until it, too, was put down by Soviet tanks. The regime that eventually emerged, though Communist, also gradually began to loosen its ties with the Kremlin.

In Romania the reaction was much slower—probably because the Romanian economy was less developed and more dependent on Soviet aid. But eventually in Bucharest, too, nationalist sentiment increased and with it resistance to Soviet efforts to dominate the economy.

Even in Czechoslovakia a fresh wind began to blow. Enjoying perhaps the most advanced economy, the Czechs were among the first to suffer from a system designed for a much more primitive stage of development, and Czech economists began in 1964 to urge the adoption of a system startlingly resembling a free-market economy.

WITH this drive for more economic autonomy came an inevitable tendency for greater political independence, spurred and abetted by Moscow's troubles with Peking.

Beyond the borders of the once-monolithic Communist empire the disintegration proceeded even faster. The Communist parties of Western Europe openly criticized the parent organization in Moscow. In neutral countries the Communist parties were riddled with rivalry between Peking and Moscow factions. And in underdeveloped countries rivalry between Peking's agents and Moscow's severely weakened both.

Thus in the space of little more than a decade, the empire that Stalin had left behind was split into quarreling camps. Nevertheless, each camp continued to demonstrate its orthodoxy by vociferous denunciation of the so-called "capitalist" world—the democracies of the West and, particularly, the United States. They disagreed on the means of achieving world Communism, but each remained dedicated to that goal.

*One of the last of the doomed Romanov czars, Alexander II, is crowned with elaborate ceremony in the Kremlin in 1856.*

# Panoply of High Power

An arrogant autocracy first pulled the lands of the Russias together. The czars ruled in the name of God and with the aid of dazzling display—as well as bureaucratic brutality. The Communists, in turn, asserted a new atheistic ideology and awed their subjects with parades of power and police brutality. This traditional centralization of power proved useful to the Communists in helping them realize their expansionist foreign policy objectives. It also permitted them to begin the task of forging a modern state from the feudal empire they had wrenched from the czars.

**THE PINNACLE OF POWER,** Moscow's Kremlin looms in the golden light of waning day. Its name means fortress, and in the 13th Century it had wooden walls. These were later replaced by stone and brick, with watchtowers like that in the foreground. Over the centuries the Kremlin acquired many sacred buildings. The Cathedral of the

Annunciation (*far left*) and the Cathedral of the Archangel Michael (*left center*) are now museums. The tallest
tower (*center background*) is named for Ivan the Great, and
because Napoleon shelled it in 1812 it has been familiarly
known as "Ivan the Slightly Tipsy." At far right, outside the Kremlin, is St. Basil's Cathedral, also a museum.

HEIRLOOMS *of a turbulent*
*and splendid past are treasured*
*in the Kremlin in the*
*spirit enunciated by the writer*
*Maxim Gorki: "Citizens,*
*do not touch one stone . . . all this*
*is your history, your pride"*

ANNIVERSARY SOUVENIR, the egg above was fashioned in 1913 by the jeweler Fabergé to mark the 300 years of rule by the Romanov dynasty.

CZAR'S BEDROOM in the Terem Palace (*left*) retains its 17th Century elegance. The dynamic Peter the Great slept in its ornately carved, canopied bed.

CZARS' STUDY, the Golden Room (*opposite*) has an almost barbaric grandeur. Here the czars received their nobles. The windowpanes are stained mica.

KAZAN CROWN of gold and turquoise, topped by a topaz, was made in 1553 to mark the capture of Kazan on the Volga.

*The Great Hall in the Palace of Facets, where huge chandeliers light the vaulted*

IVORY THRONE, taken to Moscow by a Byzantine princess who wed Ivan III in 1472, was used in coronations until 1896.

**SCEPTER AND ORB**, laden with gems, were made in Constantinople in the 17th Century. The orb has a great ruby in its cross.

*ceilings and make the floor shimmer, was once the scene of imperial receptions.*

**DIAMOND THRONE**, also used for coronations, sparkles with 2,000 diamonds and amethysts. It came from Persia in 1660.

# THE MAILED FIST, *brusquely displayed in Moscow, long served to keep the satellite nations under Soviet sway*

POWER DISPLAY is presented by massed Soviet Army soldiers (*opposite*) marching past Lenin's image in Red Square to celebrate the anniversary of the Bolshevik Revolution.

MILITARY MIGHT of Russia strikes in Budapest in 1956 as a Soviet tank roars into the city to crush the Hungarian rebellion. Insurgents until then had been in control.

HOSPITABLE BALINESE greet Nikita Khrushchev (*above*) during an extensive Asian tour undertaken by the Soviet Premier in 1960 to promote economic agreements.

SMILING LEADER, Premier Wladyslaw Gomulka of Poland (*right, with glasses*) welcomes Russian Party Chairman Leonid Brezhnev on his arrival in January 1965.

STERN RIVAL, Chou En-lai, the Premier of China (*below, fourth from left*), foe of Russia's coexistence policy, meets his visitor, Premier Aleksei Kosygin, in February 1965.

ASIAN GUEST, India's Prime Minister Lal Bahadur Shastri arrives in Moscow (*opposite*) in May 1965. Shastri came at the invitation of the Soviet Union seven months after Khrushchev was deposed. By such overtures, the Russians have been trying to strengthen their ties with the underdeveloped nations.

*Carrying Stalin's coffin in 1953 are (from right) Beria, Malenkov, Vasily Stalin, Molotov, Bulganin and Kaganovich. Khrushchev*

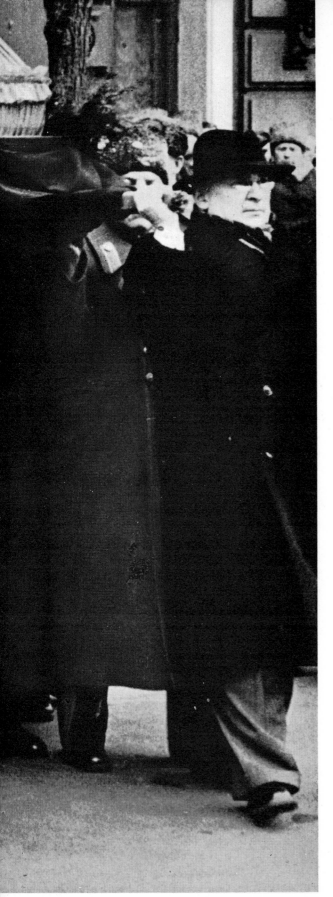

*(behind coffin) demoted them all and was himself ousted in 1964.*

# 3

# Changing Shape of Party Rule

THE Communist Party, the repository of ul-timate power in the Soviet Union, is not a party at all in the Western sense. It is not a mass political organization, with many voting adher-ents and relatively few active members, but a small, highly select band of men and women who rule the country with great power. Accord-ing to party statutes, the party has two func-tions: to determine high policy for the U.S.S.R. and to supervise the implementation of that policy. Today the party has close to 12 million members, of both full and candidate status. The membership represents about 5 per cent of the population and is made up primarily of work-ers, farmers, Government officials, managers, engineers, and Army and secret-police officers. It also includes some students. About 200,000 members are full-time, paid functionaries. They constitute the core of the party's apparatus.

The organizational principle of the party, as once set forth by Lenin, is "democratic central-ism." This contradiction in terms (democracy equals rule by the people, but centralism equals rule by the center) means that authority comes from the top. Lenin in fact stated that the proletariat, in whose name he claimed to rule, could not determine policy. They must be led.

IN theory the highest organ of the Communist Party is the party Congress. This body is required by law to convene every four years, but frequently it meets more often. Aside from approving what the leadership has done between sessions, the Congress is supposed to "determine the tactical line of the party on major questions of current policy." But in actuality the Congress seldom debates policy questions.

In the intervals between meetings of the Congress, the party's Central Committee ostensibly makes policy and directs the Soviet Government. This body, with 181 voting members in 1965, currently convenes two or more times each year. The Central Committee maintains bureaus for supervising every phase of national life. There are bureaus for the Army, for heavy industry, light industry, foreign policy, the arts, propaganda, finances, youth and, most important of all, personnel. This last group handles the promotion, demotion or transfer of all top party officials, while the other sections control industrial, military and governmental policy and appointments. The various sections are directed by members of the Central Secretariat of the party, which meets daily to handle current political and administrative problems and which reports directly to the party leadership.

At the top of the pyramid of Soviet power is the Presidium (previously called the Politburo), which has varied greatly in size over the years but presently numbers 11 members. Here the most important questions of Soviet policy, involving hundreds of millions of people, are thrashed out and decided in complete secrecy. During much of Stalin's regime the dictator decided all policy questions himself. But except for this period the Presidium has always been the party's ruling body.

While the party makes all policies, it does not directly administer them. Administration is in the hands of the Soviet Government, which stands parallel to, but separate from, the party apparatus. The Government is organized along more conventional lines, beginning with local *soviets*, or councils, and their executive units and rising through the governments of the republics (roughly comparable to U.S. states) to the Supreme Soviet, which is the national legislature, and its executive, the Council of Ministers. The chairman of the Council of Ministers is the premier, the formal head of the Soviet national Government.

The task of the Government officials is to carry out the policies originated by the party. Throughout the Soviet Union the Government operates through a series of industrial ministries and geographic subdivisions. The latter consist of republics, autonomous republics and regions (ethnic and territorial subdivisions of republics), and lesser subdivisions down to the *rayon*, or county. These units are frequently shifted about to correspond with geographic, racial and functional requirements much as any large business organization shifts its component parts to deal with changing problems.

DESPITE its seeming cumbersomeness and the duality of "party" and "Government," the system has advantages. Chief among them is that it relieves the makers of policy from the routine of administration, leaving them free to ponder policy matters. But the policy makers have not always wanted to be free of administrative matters, and the duality has not always been maintained. In 1958 Khrushchev, then First Secretary of the party, ousted Nikolai Bulganin from the premiership and had himself elected to the post. He thus held supreme authority in the party and the state. The separation was restored after his dismissal, when Aleksei Kosygin became Premier of the Government and Leonid Brezhnev First Secretary of the party.

Along with its advantages the system of dual authority has its drawbacks. On every level of Government, from the Council of Ministers to the lowest factory board, the party representative upholds the political point of view for which he has been trained. His counterpart, on the other hand—the minister, the manager, the engineer or the scientist—is primarily concerned with technical operations. The supremacy of the party has in the past been clear enough to suppress any resentments the technical class may feel against political interference. But the possibility of friction always remains.

THEORETICALLY all party officials and all principal officers of the Government are elected by secret ballot. In practice they are appointed by the party organs above them. Who then appoints the leader or leaders at the very top? The absence of any Constitutional provision for selecting these officials is probably the gravest defect in the Soviet power structure, as has been demonstrated by the ups and downs of Russian political history since the Revolution.

Before the Revolution, Lenin was confronted with unruly majorities against him. But he was able to maintain his leadership—in part by his dominating personality, ability and charisma; in part by improvisation; and in part, too, by reinterpreting or contravening the rules that he and his comrades had previously agreed upon.

Stalin, who lacked Lenin's personality and popularity, resorted to much more devious methods to reach the top and used brute terror to remain there. His method was to exploit all the possibilities of his position as First Secretary of the party. The technique is relatively simple. At every level of party organization the secretary in charge has two functions: to nominate and appoint subordinate personnel and to determine the questions and hence the answers to be dealt with at party gatherings. Since all the secretaries are nominated and appointed by a superior party echelon, a First Secretary who has been prudent enough to appoint adherents to key posts down the line can usually count on them to send equally faithful adherents to the various committees, conferences and congresses back up the line.

For example, during the period immediately following Lenin's death, Stalin and Trotsky were engaged in a power struggle. Although

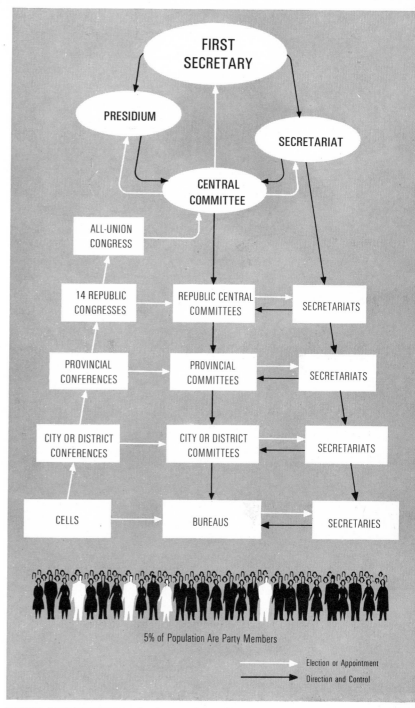

**PARTY ORGANIZATION** is shown above. By 1965 the party had more than 11 million members. All of them belong to cells. Each echelon has its own committee or bureau comprising its leadership and its secretariat. At each level the secretary (who rules the secretariat) controls the group that selected him and can control elections to the next echelon. But he is confirmed and controlled by secretaries above him, up to First Secretary.

many leading Bolsheviks disliked Stalin and opposed his policies, the young First Secretary had friends in key secretarial posts throughout the power structure. At one crucial point the party rank and file elected delegates to regional conferences of whom 36 per cent (a formidable bloc) supported Trotsky. But efficient nomination of Stalinist candidates by the regional secretaries reduced the pro-Trotsky delegates to a mere 18 per cent at the next highest level, and by the time the delegates at the top echelon had been chosen, the Trotsky supporters were no more than an insignificant minority.

THESE ruses, which brought Stalin to power, were sufficient to keep him there until the early 1930s. But then serious party opposition arose to the inhuman measures he had instituted during his industrialization and collectivization drives, and he had to resort to much more ruthless tactics to maintain discipline.

The result was the Great Purge—perhaps the most brutal period in all Russian history. Thousands of Old Bolsheviks were arrested, tortured, and forced to make humiliating and absurd confessions of plotting against the party. In three widely publicized trials more than 50 major leaders were convicted and sentenced to death, and hundreds of others were shot or exiled without trial. Scientists, artists, writers and leaders in every field were killed or banished. From 1936 to 1938 more than one third of the party was purged. So many Army officers were affected that by the start of World War II the officer corps had been decimated and Stalin had to recall men from exile in order to staff the Army. One of these was Konstantin Rokossovski, who had been purged in 1937. Rokossovski became commander of the Don front in 1943 and was twice made a Hero of the Soviet Union. In 1944 he was made a marshal—the highest rank in the Soviet Army. By the time the purge was over, hundreds of thousands had been arrested and either liquidated or banished to slave labor camps.

During the purges Stalin raised an almost impenetrable curtain between the Soviet Union and the outside world. The Russian people were cut off from all contact with foreigners and all access to foreign publications. Any Soviet citizen found conversing with a foreigner was automatically suspect, and a Russian who caught sight of a foreign friend approaching on the sidewalk usually darted away in panic.

ONE consequence was that for the rest of Stalin's lifetime the party was virtually eliminated as a policy-making body. An absolute dictator with a phenomenal grasp of detail, Stalin ruled without the party, using whatever channels were available. His secret police, then known as the NKVD, were often entrusted with running whole branches of industry.

The outbreak of World War II brought some relief from the terror but no relaxation of Stalin's personal grip. Nor did the end of the war and the victory bring any respite. Exhausted by four years of effort and worn down by the constant strain of Stalin's incessant threatening, the people looked forward to some easing of controls and to greater incentives. But Stalin never let down. Instead he drove the Russian people harder than ever to rebuild their cities and to rehabilitate their factories. During the war the peasants had been free from strict supervision as long as they met their production quotas. Now they were gathered together again into the hated collective system.

Early in 1953 Stalin ordered the arrest of a group of doctors on the charge of plotting to kill high Soviet officials by the use of improper medical treatment. The men around him feared another purge. But the crisis was short-lived. On a cold day in March the head of Stalin's bodyguard telephoned the top party lieutenants, Vyacheslav Molotov, Georgi Malenkov, Nikita Khrushchev and the police chief, Lavrenty Beria, to announce that the dictator had had a stroke. Stalin lingered for a few days, but on March 6, 1953, it was announced that he had died the night before.

"I wept," Khrushchev later told a foreign visitor. "Like Peter he fought barbarism with barbarism. But he was a great man."

Dazed and not a little terrified at the prospect of assuming Stalin's awesome role, his followers appealed to the party and the people not to panic. Then they faced the problem for which their system has no ready solution: how to select a successor.

The temporary expedient they hit upon was "collective leadership." At first it consisted of a quadrumvirate composed of Malenkov, Molotov, Beria and Khrushchev. Malenkov, as Premier, was "first among equals." Soon after, in fear that Beria's control of the police would enable him to assume power for himself, his colleagues had the police chief dismissed from office and expelled from the party. By the end of the year he had been shot.

HAVING disposed of Beria, the leadership pledged not to liquidate each other any more. At the same time, in an effort to win popularity and confidence, they began to relax the pressures under which the Russian people had suffered for a generation. The police were restricted and brought under the control of the Government. Many political prisoners were freed, and the living conditions of those remaining in the concentration camps were greatly improved. Finally, in a famous 1956 speech, Khrushchev openly denounced his former master for the barbarism of his reign.

Working through the Government apparatus, Malenkov introduced plans to raise the standard of living by increasing the production of consumer goods. Khrushchev, who was First Secretary of the party, turned his attention to the rickety party structure and began to reorganize it. Shrewdly aping the methods of the master he had denounced, Khrushchev put his own adherents in key posts all the way down the line, strengthening his personal position and elbowing his colleagues out of power.

Malenkov was forced out as Premier and was replaced by Bulganin, whose position as Minister of Defense was given to Marshal Georgi Zhukov. In 1958, three years after he assumed the premiership, Bulganin resigned and Khrushchev succeeded him.

By 1957 Khrushchev's opponents had recognized the threat he presented and they demanded his ouster. But it was too late. Invoking a long-ignored party statute, Khrushchev appealed to the Central Committee over the heads of the majority of his Presidium colleagues and ordered its members to convene in Moscow. He also enlisted the support of Defense Minister Zhukov, who airlifted dozens of Khrushchev's supporters into Moscow from all over the country to attend the crucial meeting. The anti-Khrushchev majority in the Presidium was turned into a helpless minority in the full committee. Malenkov and Molotov were expelled from the party and were sent away from Moscow to minor posts in the hinterlands. "A mathematical majority," Khrushchev later joked somewhat cynically, "can often become a political minority."

But the stratagem was highly risky. If Khrushchev conceded the right of the Central Committee to name the ruler of the U.S.S.R., what was to prevent his colleagues from using the same tactic to oust him at some future date?

As we shall see, Khrushchev's rule was uneven —sometimes successful, sometimes disastrous. At first he won enormous prestige by raising living standards and pursuing a highly vigorous diplomacy abroad. But then his schemes began to falter. His promises of phenomenal improvements in the economy and in agriculture proved as illusory as Stalin's had been. His prestige dwindled in the face of such humiliating defeats as the Cuban venture and his ineffective handling of the Chinese Communists.

BY 1964 Khrushchev's reputation and his program were at a low ebb. Yet his position seemed unassailable. Resentful of Khrushchev's highhanded manner and aware that he could no longer count on the support of many of his earlier followers, some of his colleagues in the Presidium began to plot his downfall.

Although the details of the plot are not yet known, its outlines are clear. While Khrushchev was relaxing at his Black Sea villa in October 1964, the plotters called secret meetings of both the Presidium and the Central Committee, issuing invitations to all those known to be opposed to Khrushchev but neglecting to ask his supporters. At the Presidium meeting, party theorist Mikhail Suslov detailed Khrushchev's failures in a long polemic. The result was a unanimous vote against Khrushchev. The situation in the Central Committee was more delicate. There the anti-Khrushchev forces could muster only a bare majority. But that was enough.

An emissary was sent to bring Khrushchev back to Moscow, where Suslov recounted the old man's sins to him. Although Khrushchev was permitted to defend himself, before both the Presidium and the full committee, his attempts were unsuccessful. After a nightlong session he offered his resignation.

In due course Brezhnev and Kosygin were installed in office. Khrushchev was denounced for his "immature conclusions and hasty decisions," and vanished into the obscurity of one of the Moscow housing complexes that he had envisaged as monuments to his benign reign.

The method of choosing a ruler of Russia has recently become considerably less gory. Although shorn of power, Khrushchev appeared in public to cast his vote in a Moscow election in 1965. But the lines of succession are far from clear. A change of government in the Soviet Union remains what it has always been—a risky business of plot, conspiracy and coup d'état.

THE future of the party also remains unclear. Many of the members of the Presidium had not reached their teens when the Revolution occurred and one was not even born. Stalin and Khrushchev were battle-scarred veterans; they are not. But the top leaders received their training under Stalin, and both Brezhnev and Kosygin were close to the dictator until his death. Although these older men are committed to an anti-Stalinist line, they are strict disciplinarians by training and experience.

The young party recruits of today have a different background and may turn out to be a somewhat different breed. The starting point for the Communist leaders of the future is the Komsomol, or Young Communist League. Here those with political ambitions are trained and tested. In the early years the recruit is expected to devote a good deal of time to party work, organizing meetings, delivering speeches and doing odd jobs for the local party.

Nowadays, with more opportunities available for leisure-time entertainment, not all Soviet youth relish the burdens of party membership. Moreover, recognizing the risks of high position, many of them prefer to stand aside from political life and to devote themselves to careers as engineers, doctors or scientists.

Finally, in the puritanical society of Russia today the party member is expected to be the most puritanical of all. While others may occasionally get drunk, skip a day's work or even go to church, the party member is required to set an example of Soviet morality. If he fails to do so he can expect to lose his party card.

FOR these reasons the successful young party member is generally a dedicated, mentally agile careerist with considerable administrative experience. If he has demonstrated these qualities, the chances are that he will be sent to a special school to study party doctrine and the techniques of government. Later he will be assigned as a party secretary to some remote area. Frequent transfers are the rule, and before he finally reaches national prominence he will have served in a dozen towns and cities throughout the country.

By the time he has become a member of the Central Committee or the Presidium, the party member has gone through a rigorous training and several party schools, which have made him a devoted official, a disciplined political soldier and a selfless servant of his cause.

The re-emergence of the party, the potential upgrading of the Central Committee and the change in party membership do not signify any great democratization of the Soviet Government. They merely demonstrate that the structure of power in the Soviet Union is not immutable. Indeed, it seems never to stop changing.

*The two most powerful forces in the development of the party, Lenin and Stalin, meet together outside Moscow in 1922.*

# The Party's Leaders and Ranks

Lenin organized and developed the Communist Party as a tightly disciplined body dedicated to the principle of revolution. Orders came from the top but the leadership was somewhat responsive to new ideas initiated from below, provided these did not disturb the centralization of power. Stalin remade the party into his own instrument, then later virtually ignored it. Khrushchev, though originally a disciple of Stalin, reverted to the Lenin concept of "party democracy" and, before he was ousted in 1964, revivified the party as a means of governing the state.

55

# MEMBERSHIP *in the party is a highly prized privilege in the Soviet Union*

**HONORING LENIN,** delegates to the 22nd Party Congress march in Moscow (*above*) toward the tomb of the Soviet Union's first ruler. The party has cells in virtually every enterprise.

**AWAITING A CEREMONY,** youngsters about to be made members of the Young Pioneers, the party's children's organization, self-consciously line up in front of the Kremlin (*opposite*).

**APPLYING TO JOIN,** a hopeful worker, Mikhail Dedushko, appears before a Rostov cell (*right*) to tell its officers why he believes he has the qualifications for membership in the party.

IN 1937 Stalin (*above, second from right*) stands next to Premier Vyacheslav Molotov (*right*) at a parade. A new figure, Khrushchev, stood two places to Stalin's right.

IN 1962 Khrushchev, undisputed ruler since 1958, leads a retinue that includes Leonid Brezhnev (*below, bottom right*) and Aleksei Kosygin (*behind Brezhnev*).

AT THE PINNACLE OF POWER, the leaders of the new Soviet regime that had just deposed Khrushchev appear together publicly for the first time. The occasion

was a 1964 rally in Red Square honoring Soviet Cosmonauts. From left to right are Kosygin, who succeeded Khrushchev as Premier; Nikolai Podgorny, a member of the Presidium; Brezhnev, who took over Khrushchev's position as the First Secretary of the Communist Party; and Anastas Mikoyan, President of the Presidium.

*A technician, Viktor Terekhov, mans the control panel of a deoxidizing line at the big Novolipetsky Steel Plant 300 miles south of Moscow,*

*one of the most highly automated steel plants in the world.*

# 4

# A State-Run Economy

HOW has the Communist planned economy worked in comparison with capitalism? Soviet economists point out that the United States took about 60 years, from 1850 to 1910, to create a mature industrial economy, whereas by their reckoning they accomplished the same task in half the time, beginning in 1929 and ending in the early 1950s.

Western economists, however, suggest that Russian industrialization actually began at the end of the 19th Century and that by World War I the country had a substantial production of such basic goods as coal, steel and oil. Though most of the factories lay idle during the Revolution and the subsequent civil war, the machinery, manpower and technical experience were nonetheless at hand when the Bolsheviks got around to resuming the country's march toward industrialization. Therefore, say these economists, the rate of Russian industrialization has been more or less the same as that of all the other countries undergoing a similar development—except that the cost in lives and hardships to the Russian population has been incomparably greater than it has been in any non-Communist country. This was due largely to the methods chosen by the Bolsheviks after they took power in 1917.

While Karl Marx laid down many specific rules for setting up a Communist state politically, he did not give his followers any advice on how to organize a socialist economy. As Lenin himself said during the Revolution: "We have knowledge of socialism, but as for knowledge of . . . the organization and distribution of commodities—that we have not. This the old Bolshevik leaders did not teach us. . . ."

Improvising as he went along, Lenin first invited the old factory managers to stay on the job as employees of the state. But the managers' response was unenthusiastic. This left most of the plants in the hands of untrained party members. With the onset of the civil war, production rapidly declined, consumer goods all but disappeared, and the currency became almost worthless.

NEVERTHELESS, Lenin proclaimed that the state was being run on Marxist principles. The attempt to meet recurring crises was dubbed "War Communism." Since the population's most pressing need was for food, which the peasantry alone produced, Lenin ordered the peasants to deliver all surplus supplies to requisitioning gangs from the cities and to accept almost worthless money in payment. Many peasants refused; the city markets lay empty and famine spread. In an effort to feed the Russian population the United States sent in large quantities of food through the American Relief Administration under Herbert Hoover. But still the toll in lives reached staggering figures.

By 1921, surrounded by evidence of the complete breakdown of War Communism, Lenin finally ordered a temporary retreat and introduced his "New Economic Policy," whereby at least some small manufacturing and retailing enterprises were returned to private hands and peasants were permitted to trade their grain for manufactured goods. Conditions improved quickly, and the peasants, once again able to buy the goods they needed, began selling their food to the cities. By 1926 the prewar industrial production level had been reached.

But at that rate the industrialization of the country, which Lenin's successor Stalin considered essential for Communist survival, would obviously be slow indeed. Stalin also knew, moreover, that the sweeping program he envisaged would require a ruthless dictatorship. Not until 1927 had he established himself firmly enough in power to begin plans for his program.

LIKE the head of any nation attempting to build a modern industrial state, Stalin faced tremendous problems. In order to achieve the ambitious goals set forth in the First Five-Year Plan of 1928, he had to accumulate capital to construct the plants and factories he needed. He also had to develop a reservoir of technological skills, to establish a system for allocating raw materials and to obtain workers for the new factories. Unable to lure foreign investors to risk capital in revolutionary Russia, he was forced to resort to taxing his own subjects, in part by forced loans but chiefly by selling consumer goods at enormous markups —a form of enforced sales tax. To this day, if a Soviet woman needs, say, four yards of plain, unbleached white cotton to make a new work smock, she may have to pay as much as 70 cents a yard for it—or $2.80. Since cost figures are usually secret in the Soviet economy, she does not know that the cotton cost the Government only 20 cents a yard to produce, or 80 cents for the four yards she purchased. The remaining two dollars that she had to pay is simply a tax and probably will be used to help finance a new factory or, perhaps, a new rocket to the moon.

In building a technological base Stalin was able to take advantage of the technical advances already achieved by the more developed countries of the West. In the late 1920s and early 1930s hundreds of engineers and technicians from Europe and America went to Russia, bringing with them the latest industrial techniques of the West. In 1932 Colonel Hugh Cooper, an American, completed on the Dnieper River Russia's first big modern hydroelectric power plant. Engineers from the Ford Motor Company were hired to teach the Soviet automobile industry to use mass-production techniques.

Nonetheless, a shortage of foreign currency sharply limited Stalin's ability to buy Western machinery and technical assistance, and he was forced to rely largely on native sources of money and talent. When the First Five-Year Plan was launched Russia was still dependent on foreign sources for many essential raw materials. Suspecting that his huge country contained undiscovered resources of its own, Stalin placed a high priority on the education of mineralogists and the development of prospecting methods. Within a decade teams of trained geologists were traversing the country and locating deposits of many of the resources that Soviet industry needed.

AT the same time Stalin launched a crash program to expand Russia's educational facilities, particularly in the fields of engineering and the sciences. Universities, polytechnic institutes, night and correspondence schools were expanded enormously, and adult party members were urged to attend them. Today most of the top Soviet leaders and factory managers are graduates of the educational institutions that Stalin either founded or enlarged. Leonid Brezhnev, for example, was 29 when he was graduated from a metallurgical institute. Aleksei Kosygin is a graduate of a textile institute. But when the Five-Year Plan first got under way in the early '30s, most of the men Stalin put in charge of his big plants were simply loyal party members who had had little or no technical training.

For his labor force Stalin initially had little difficulty luring young people from the unpopular collective farms he had organized in the countryside. At first the young laborers, spurred by visions of a plentiful life at the end of the Five-Year Plan, worked hard. But as the luster of Stalin's unfulfilled promises wore off, they became disillusioned, and Stalin had to resort to force to bring in additional workers to overcome the lethargy of the overworked, underpaid laborers. Introducing piecework wage scales—one of the worst features of early capitalism—he periodically raised work norms, lowered wages, prescribed heavy fines for tardiness and ordered prison terms for absenteeism. For those who failed to conform, he built huge slave labor camps in the wastes of Siberia. Revulsion against these demonic methods among all classes—including party politicians, factory managers, members of the intelligentsia, workers and peasants—possibly constituted a major justification, in Stalin's mind, for the terrible terror and purges of the mid-1930s that took thousands of lives.

Despite the extreme shortage of consumer goods that characterized the entire Stalin period, the dictator stuck stubbornly to his goal of building heavy industry—above all, steel. Light industry, housing, agriculture, services, all were held back in favor of the steel mills and factories that turned out the machinery and weapons Stalin insisted on.

The chief characteristic of Stalin's industrial organization was centralized control, a function chiefly performed by the party. Every factory, plant and institution had its party cell that watched over the management and reported the shortcomings of all levels—from managerial to that of the lowliest laborer—to party headquarters.

THE planning apparatus was headed by GOSPLAN, the State Planning Committee, whose function it was to translate Stalin's ambitious goals into production schedules for every enterprise in the Soviet Union, as well as to allocate labor, raw materials and investment funds for each.

In practice a number of separate programs were incorporated into GOSPLAN's master plan. One gave the quotas for annual production and was the main program to be observed by plant managers. The Five-Year, or sometimes Seven-Year, Plan that consolidated the annual plans was primarily a propaganda device designed to spur production and provide evidence of the giant strides being made in Soviet development. Occasionally, when things went well, Stalin would arbitrarily decree that a Five-Year Plan be compressed into a shorter period. Thereupon production quotas for every plant and every worker would be stepped up. If, on the other hand, production lagged, the statistics were doctored to make it appear that the plan had been fulfilled.

Such doctoring was resorted to both by planners at the top and by plant managers who feared for their hides if their production fell short. The result was that over the years Soviet statistics became such a jumble of myth and reality that the planners themselves were ignorant of the actual state of the economy they were assigned to supervise. There were other difficulties as well. When the plant managers were handed their plan they had little or nothing to say about where they should buy their raw material, how much to pay their labor or even what processes they were to use in turning out their products. Such matters had already been arranged under the plan, and the managers' only function was to allocate to each subdivision in the factory its share of the plan and to insist that the quotas be fulfilled.

ABOVE all the workers, the managers and the planners sat Stalin—exhorting, cursing and threatening. No plant manager was too far from Moscow to escape the dreaded midnight phone calls from the center and hear the voice of the old man in the Kremlin scolding him for some failure to fulfill the current plan. And in every enterprise Stalin's party minions pried into all aspects of the production drive, reporting lapses by the technicians, shortfalls in production, mismanagement and laxness—urging that more effort be put into everything except the welfare of the workers in whose name, of

course, the gigantic effort was being made.

Although the toll in suffering, deprivation and hardship for the Soviet workers was severe, by and large the system worked. Soviet production of steel and other basic industrial items grew at a prodigious rate. Taking advantage of technological progress already made in more advanced countries, of an unlimited and disciplined (if unskilled) labor force and rich natural resources, the technicians succeeded in rapidly creating a functioning industrial economy on the base they had been bequeathed.

DESPITE the fact that the system itself was cumbersome and rigid, the simplicity of Stalin's production goals—more steel, more iron, more coal and more oil—made it possible to overcome the drawbacks of Soviet central planning. Moreover, because of the centralized control, Stalin had the added advantage of being able to concentrate his resources on whatever sector he chose. He had at his disposal an army of thoroughly trained engineers and technicians, scientists and designers, thanks to his earlier concentration on education. When the United States confronted him with the atom bomb, for example, Stalin was able to launch a crash program that produced a bomb more quickly than might have been possible in a more loosely organized system. Similarly, Stalin was able to launch a major drive in rocketry and achieve an apparent head start which the Soviet Union was able to maintain until the mid-1960s.

Thanks also to his foresight in training prospectors to search for the hidden resources of Russia, he was able to find and produce many of the rare ores and raw minerals needed in modern industry.

But, as the needs of the nation became more refined and varied, the task of the central planners became vastly more intricate. It was one thing to plan the production of so many tons of steel from iron and coal; it was quite another thing to plan a complex economy to deal with the demands of different groups within the society.

When Stalin died, the Soviet's leaders quickly recognized that the entire system required renovation. Georgi Malenkov, who emerged as Stalin's first successor, tried to win popularity and raise morale by promises of more consumer goods and better housing. But the production system Stalin had left made no provision for meeting such goals; the machines to make the consumer goods had first to be designed and produced, and the building material for new housing had first to be found.

Before Malenkov could make good his extravagant promises he was ousted by Khrushchev. Although Khrushchev had attacked Malenkov for slighting heavy industry, within a few years he, too, began to curry popularity by promising that the Soviet economy soon would overtake that of the United States in consumer goods and food.

THE fundamental problem that faced Khrushchev was how to stimulate the lagging sectors of the Russian economy and enable them to catch up with the more advanced sectors, without destroying gains that had been made. His basic approach was to reorganize the managerial structure, at first decentralizing, then recentralizing. He instituted reforms designed to give more initiative to managers and to free them from the constant interference of the central planners. He encouraged them to try innovations and to copy the newest techniques of foreign industry.

Dismantling many of the ministries that had grown up in Moscow to direct every sector of the economy, he divided the country into more than a hundred economic districts, each one presided over by an Economic Council with considerable power to supervise planning, procurement and production in its geographic area. The councils were permitted to delegate some of their powers to factory managers. The councils' plans nevertheless remained subject to the approval of GOSPLAN in Moscow.

Khrushchev's decentralization was an extremely controversial innovation, and it was opposed by many men high in the Kremlin,

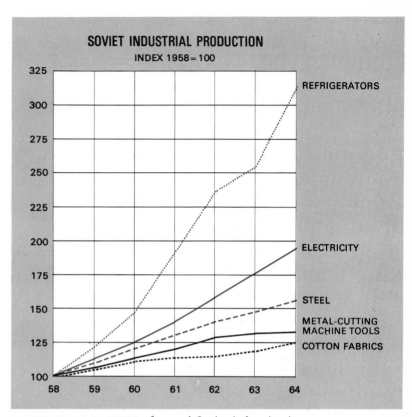

PRODUCTION GROWTH of several Soviet industries is shown on the above graph (1964 figures are estimates). The growth rate for all Soviet industry was 8.5 per cent in 1963 and 7.5 per cent in the first half of 1964.

some of whom thought that increasing centralization was the answer to economic ills. Others feared that they would lose some of their power. Many of the technicians in the Moscow ministries, who were assigned to provincial towns to run the Economic Councils, were equally unhappy with the reform.

But Khrushchev could point out that only administrative authority was being decentralized. Ultimate control was still in the hands of the party representatives stationed all over the country in every factory and in every shop. These officials he encouraged to increase their vigilance and report infractions and laxness to central headquarters.

Khrushchev thus succeeded in disgruntling the Moscow bureaucrats without alleviating the basic inadequacies of the system—among them the harassments inflicted on factory managers across the country by party functionaries less technically qualified than themselves and the insistence of the over-all plan upon quantity of production rather than quality.

Nevertheless, the first results of Khrushchev's reforms appeared to be encouraging. Partially freed from the deadening hand of the center (although not from the party controllers), some managers began to rethink their methods, to introduce new procurement procedures and to design more efficient machines. Production increased. For several years a real boom took place, and the Soviet economy grew at a spectacular rate—not only in the field of heavy industry but in those of consumer goods and housing as well.

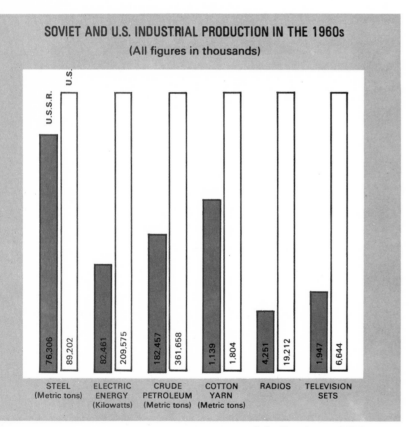

**SOVIET AND U.S. INDUSTRIAL PRODUCTION IN THE 1960s**
(All figures in thousands)

| | U.S.S.R. | U.S. |
|---|---|---|
| STEEL (Metric tons) | 76,306 | 89,202 |
| ELECTRIC ENERGY (Kilowatts) | 82,461 | 209,575 |
| CRUDE PETROLEUM (Metric tons) | 182,457 | 361,658 |
| COTTON YARN (Metric tons) | 1,139 | 1,804 |
| RADIOS | 4,251 | 19,212 |
| TELEVISION SETS | 1,947 | 6,644 |

COMPARATIVE OUTPUT of the Russian and U.S. economies is shown on the graph above. On a per capita basis, the U.S. is more productive in all categories. In 1963, for example, the Soviet Union produced about 1,705 kilowatt hours of electric power per person; the U.S. per capita output was about 5,320 kilowatt hours.

So rapid was the growth that economists abroad began to suspect that Khrushchev might make good his threat to catch up with the United States by 1970. Some American economists were disturbed by the slow growth rate of the U.S. economy compared to the Soviet Union's. Such fears proved unfounded, however, when Soviet statistics revealed that there had been a sharp decline in growth rates after 1958. Simultaneously, a boom in the U.S. increased the disparity between the two systems.

By 1964 the slowdown in the Soviet economy had become too obvious to hide. Not only had the economic growth rate dropped sharply but no consumer in the Soviet Union had to be told that his standard of living, which until then had been climbing steadily, was not rising as rapidly as Khrushchev had promised it would. Despite Khrushchev's railing and scolding at the managers, the economists and the technicians, it was apparent that his promises of overtaking the West in industrial output were pipe dreams.

Still mesmerized by Stalin's dictum that a plan must be fulfilled, and under orders from Khrushchev to operate within strictly defined budgets, factory managers sought to solve their dilemma by turning out items at the lowest cost possible. The resulting products were often shoddy.

THE consumer, meantime, once he had satisfied his most basic needs, sought better-quality goods that met his individual taste. The result was that stores began to fill with unwanted articles—bad shoes, poor textiles, unattractive dresses. But by Stalin's still prevalent standards—and even by Khrushchev's—there was no one to blame. The factory manager had fulfilled his plan and had done so within his budget. The retail stores had dutifully displayed the factories' products for sale. The fact that the consumer had refused to buy and that warehouses were jammed with unwanted commodities was no one's fault. Or was it?

Something was wrong, and Khrushchev's colleagues in the Presidium realized that he had failed to keep the economy growing. While he rested in his Black Sea summer home in 1964, they maneuvered to remove him. As soon as he had been dismissed they denounced his hare-brained schemes and his unorthodox planning methods and innovations. They in turn promised to make their decisions on the basis of objective facts and scientific methods. But whether their objective facts and scientific methods could cope successfully with the current ills of the Soviet economy remained to be seen.

Even before the Soviet economy had begun to slow down, some foreign economists had predicted that it was reaching the end of its initial growth period and that only fundamental structural changes in the system could assure its continued growth. Once the building of a heavy-industry base was completed, they contended, continued growth would depend on producing for the consumer. But, they went on to point out, the entire structure of the Soviet's centrally planned system was both politically and economically ill-adapted to operating a consumer-oriented economy.

EVEN Soviet economists were beginning to question certain fundamental aspects of the system. They pointed out that since Stalin had denounced interest as a capitalist device, managers paid no interest on the capital advanced them for their enterprises. Consequently, not only was capital relatively unproductive, but neither managers nor planners reckoned it as a part of production costs. Therefore it was almost impossible to figure actual costs.

Soviet economists also criticized the Stalinist dogma that plan fulfillment—that is, output figures—should be the main criterion on which a plant's performance should be based. In its place they suggested that profits on invested capital should be the chief index of achievement. They also suggested that prices respond to the market forces of supply and demand and that government should indeed charge interest on the use of capital by shops and factories. The foremost proponent of these novel ideas was the Kharkov economist Evsei Liberman.

Even under Khrushchev experiments had been started which were designed to improve the quality of consumer goods and to halt the accumulation of unsalable articles. Two factories in the clothing industry were authorized to draw up their production schedules in response to the orders for specific items that they received from retail stores rather than on the basis of orders received from the central planners. Thus, if consumers indicated a preference for certain items, the store managers could place orders for them and the factory managers would produce them at a price that had been agreed upon between them. The innovation proved such a success that 400 consumer-goods plants and their suppliers were allowed to adopt the system.

Yet this radically new approach scarcely constituted a cure-all for the many troubles besetting the Soviet economy. In the first place it involved only a tiny fraction of Soviet production. In the second place the effectiveness of the new system inevitably was limited by arbitrarily planned production levels somewhere along the line. For example, if Soviet consumers showed a preference for a certain type of textile and store managers placed large orders with textile plants for it, the plant managers in turn would have to acquire the raw materials and the machines to produce it in sufficient quantities to meet the demand. In turn the manufacturers of the looms or of the fibers would require orders for increased production of those items. Somewhere, consumers' demands would come into conflict with the plan's production figures.

THE political implications of the innovation may be even more profound. Prime Minister Benjamin Disraeli of Britain once remarked: "In politics experiments mean revolutions." If plant managers were free to plan and produce on the basis of orders from consumers, what would happen to the party controllers who previously had enjoyed the final say in every factory? The Soviet economic system leaves few decisions to the discretion of the individual. To leave even a fraction of productive capacity dependent upon the individual tastes of consumers involves a sharp reorientation in the outlook of every party official involved. Furthermore, if the consumer enjoyed the small discretion granted him, what was to prevent his asking for more in wider fields?

The dream of every Soviet citizen is to own a car. Khrushchev, like Stalin, adamantly refused to develop an automobile industry for a mass market. The masses, he said, should have their fun in buses. He even, according to his successors, forbade many busy plant managers to use cars for official business. The result was, as at least one high Soviet official later pointed out, that the managers were forced to resort to the illegal use of trucks to get around.

THE automobile problem illustrates one of the basic dilemmas of the present Soviet rulers. They could not promise cars to consumers without allocating the enormous resources needed for an automobile economy— not just the steel for construction but the spare parts to maintain the cars, the gasoline and the fuel stations to distribute it, the roads, and the cement and labor to build and maintain the roads. Yet the Soviet rulers are beginning to recognize that they must in the end consider the consumer and use the nation's resources to satisfy his demands if they are to continue to develop their economy. But to do so may mean abdicating in large measure their heretofore undisputed economic power in favor of the individual's preference. Furthermore, they must allocate sufficient resources to satisfy at least a substantial part of the demand.

But their resources are limited, and the rival claimants to those resources and to the amounts of surplus capital that are available are as demanding as is the consumer. These claimants are the proponents of giving continued priority to heavy industry—men brought up and trained in the Stalin tradition and who fear the implication of radical change. They also include members of the military, which needs heavy industry not only to produce guns

and airplanes but also to produce the intricate machines required to make modern missiles. The claimants also number men in the space industry who demand a major share of the country's technical and scientific establishment. Finally there are the peasants, who for nearly half a century have enjoyed the lowest priority of all.

How the pie is to be divided will depend in the final analysis on the leaders in the Kremlin, but in part it will depend on the managers, technicians, scientists and economists on whose advice the Kremlin must ultimately rely.

No longer the fearful, cringing people who cowered under Stalin, these men are more and more asserting their prerogatives and demanding greater autonomy and respect for their expert judgments.

A foreign visitor to Soviet factories soon becomes accustomed to the difference between the factory manager and his party watchdog. The manager generally is soft-spoken and likes to discuss the technical difficulties his plant faces and the methods he proposes for overcoming them. The party man on the other hand is louder, apt to bluster and to resent searching questions. He likes to talk about what the factory has accomplished, its plan fulfillment figures and its happy workers.

NO signs of antagonism between the two are likely to appear as long as the foreigner is present. But when the visitor is gone, and decisions must be made—perhaps concerning suggestions for a new and better product or for a more rational process that might temporarily jeopardize production schedules or put the plant's financial books out of balance for a time—one suspects that it will be the manager who votes for innovation and the party man for leaving things as they are. In the past the party man has always been preeminent and his word has been law. But considering the dilemmas facing the Soviet economy, perhaps one day the technician's quiet voice will more often be heard above the blustering shouts of the party doctrinaire.

*A sign of Soviet progress, a giant turbine rotor is exhibited in Moscow. The rotor was made for a Volga power station.*

# Priority: Capital Goods

Massive machinery, as shown at a public fair (*above*), is impressive evidence of a Soviet economic system that emphasizes capital goods and minimizes personal consumption. The Kremlin's concentration on heavy industry is designed to support the country's large military program and to create a firm base for further economic growth. Today the emphasis has shifted somewhat in the direction of consumer production, but Western economists say that while the economy has made some great strides, Soviet economic expansion has been artificial and distorted.

**POWER RESOURCES** *are increasing as the state taps its oil fields and harnesses the Volga, still a major artery of transportation, to produce added electrical energy*

NEW POWER PLANT, with a capacity larger than America's Grand Coulee Dam, is dedicated at Kuibyshev on the Volga River (*right*). The world's largest when it opened in 1958, it was surpassed by newer plants at Volgograd and in Siberia. High-voltage lines from Kuibyshev go west to Moscow and east as far as the Urals.

**OIL DERRICKS** loom at sunset on the banks of the Caspian Sea near Baku (*left*). After the U.S., Russia is the leading oil-producing nation.

**WOOD RAFTS**, sometimes stretching half a mile in length (*above*), are used, as they have been for centuries, to float timber down the Volga.

**SILK SPINNER,** an Uzbek woman (*above*) operates modern silk-milling machinery in the fabled city of Samarkand, capital of Tamerlane's 14th Century Mongolian Empire.

**ASSEMBLY-LINE WORKERS** put together radios (*opposite*) at a plant in Tallinn, Estonia. About 42 per cent of Soviet women work, compared with 26 per cent of U.S. women.

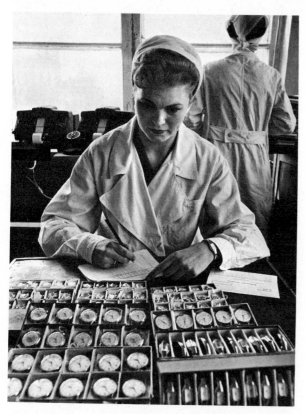

**TRACTOR BUILDERS,** employed on two seven-hour shifts a day, handle assembly-line jobs (*above*) at Minsk in Byelorussia. The factory turns out 60,000 tractors a year.

**WATCH CHECKER,** Larissa Kuzina (*left*) examines an outgoing shipment at Moscow's Watch Factory #2. The Government professes the goal of "a watch for every worker."

**INTENT TECHNICIAN** works the control apparatus (*below*) that operates 200 electrically pumped oil wells in the highly automated oil fields of the Bashkir Republic.

## CONSUMER GOODS, *long in short supply, have become increasingly available to the Soviet people in recent years*

**FREE MARKET,** located in Moscow (*right*), works on the capitalist system. Farmers from all over bring to it goods that they are permitted to produce on their own. Recently spruced up, the market has gleaming counters lined with brand-new scales.

**QUALITY FOOD,** in ever greater variety, is featured in a Leningrad store known as Gastronome #1 (*below*). Built during the last years of the czars, the store is decorated with elaborate stained-glass windows and large mirrors. It was restored in 1956.

**BIGGEST STORE** in the Soviet Union, GUM (the initials stand for "Government Department Store") has a glass-covered arcade and a fountain in Moscow (*above*). Among goods appearing in increasing quantity are television sets and refrigerators.

74

**PATRIOTIC POSTER** showing doll-like Cosmonauts is displayed at Dyetsky Mir (*above*), a Moscow children's store. In 1965 the Government directed that nearly 400 consumer-goods factories produce on the basis of demand rather than central planning.

# SPACE TRIUMPHS, *the result of heavy investment and superb technology, boost internal pride and international prestige*

**INSPECTING A ROCKET,** a young boy (*left*) gets a close look at one of the wonders of Moscow's Park of the Permanent Exhibition of Soviet Achievement. The rocket was recovered and put on display at the park after it had performed an early space mission.

WEIGHTLESS IN SPACE, Aleksei Leonov (*right*) floats away from the Voskhod II space capsule in March 1965, three months before the U.S. duplicated the feat of having a man emerge from a space capsule. In 1957 Russia shot the first artificial satellite into orbit.

MEETING THE PRESS at Moscow University in 1962 are (*from left*) Soviet Cosmonauts Gherman Titov, who orbited the earth 17 times; Yuri Gagarin, first man in space; Andrian Nikolayev, who made a twin orbit with Pavel Popovich; a scientist; and Popovich.

Kabardinian herdsmen take calves to pasture on a rolling expanse of open country in southern Russia. Government programs have

# Trial and Error on the Farm

5

*converted many seminomads into more settled livestock raisers as part of the effort to make more productive use of agricultural resources.*

OVER the centuries no problem has bedeviled the rulers of Russia more than the problem of assuring a steady flow of food for the country's population. Although it has more land than any other country in the world, Russia has only recently been able to feed itself adequately.

From the days of serfdom till the downfall of the czars, successive Governments tried a variety of remedies and reforms, but always without success. The Soviets have continued the search for a solution by herding almost the entire rural population into a nationwide system of state and collective farms.

Though collective farms are the hallmark of Russian agriculture today, outsiders rarely see them. Such secretiveness is nothing new. In the late 18th Century, when Catherine the Great wanted to visit her peasant villages her chief adviser, Grigori Potemkin, built temporary façades of fake villages in order to hide the realities of the poverty-stricken Ukrainian countryside. Today, when foreigners ask to see the collectives they are shown model communities of spanking-new barns and machine shops, neat cottages and cooperative stores. The guides label these "average farms." But the average collective is hardly as modern or well equipped. Even today some do not have electricity or running water.

In reality, the collective farm is a large, straggling village, or even several villages, with about 10,000 acres of land given over to cultivation. The houses vary in style from the black log cabins along the Siberian rivers to the flat-roofed adobe huts of Central Asia and the stone cottages of Georgia. In European Russia the houses are seldom painted and have become gray with age.

Behind each house is a shelter for the family's livestock—generally a cow, a few pigs and some chickens—and a fenced-in area known as the "private plot." On this plot, which varies in size from a half acre to two and a half acres, depending on the fertility of the soil, the owner grows vegetables for his family, fodder for his livestock and produce to sell at the nearest provincial town market.

At the highest point in the village is the church, usually dilapidated. Today it may be a storehouse or a clubhouse but sometimes it is still a house of worship. Beyond the village are the only outward signs of the collective system: a large cow barn or two for the collective herd, perhaps a silo and a shed for farm machinery, and the office building from which a state-appointed chairman rules the farm with the assistance of a dozen accountants, technicians and agronomists.

EVEN though the workers on the collective farms are supervised and regulated by the state, they do not receive a fixed salary. The peasants work the communal fields with pooled equipment, and at the end of each season the members of the collective divide the proceeds among themselves according to the amount of work each person has done, though only after the state has taken its prescribed share and after a substantial percentage of the remainder has been set aside for obligatory capital improvements. Including the income from the sale of produce grown on the private plot, the average farm family's income is about one half that of an urban family.

The poverty of Russia's farms and farmers is a measure of the failure of the Soviet Union to organize a satisfactory agricultural system. In all fairness, however, it must be said that the system is not the only villain.

A COMMON fallacy held about the Soviet Union is that its vast territory provides it with almost unlimited arable land. But in spite of its size, Russia is relatively poorly endowed with good soil for farming. In regions where the soil is good, as in the famous Black Earth areas in the Ukraine and in parts of Siberia, rainfall is often uncertain. On the other hand, in the northern areas, where there is plenty of rain, the growing season is short, and by far the largest part of Russia's arable land lies north of the 45th Parallel—roughly the latitude of Minneapolis. Moreover, most of the land area is far removed from the tempering influence of large water masses. The result is that the Soviet Union has great extremes of heat and cold. In many northern areas only the fastest-growing crops can be successfully cultivated, and such high-yield grains as winter wheat are limited largely to the southern areas of European Russia.

Added to nature's stinginess, Russian agriculture has always suffered from the rulers' deep distrust of the peasantry and their historic unwillingness to grant the peasants freedom and independence.

If, as Lenin said, the revolutionaries knew nothing about business, they knew even less about agriculture. Not one of the early Bolsheviks had had any practical experience in farming. Lenin had promised land to the peasants, and immediately after the Revolution his pledge was made good. But the factories failed to manufacture sufficient goods to exchange for farm produce. As a result the peasants no longer had any incentive to bring their grain to the markets, and famine became so acute that American relief was required. During the period of the New Economic Policy, in the early 1920s, consumer goods were available and the peasants were permitted to market their crops and livestock as they saw fit. This produced a rapid revival of the food market. But when Stalin launched his industrialization drive in 1929, it was inevitable that the earlier situation would repeat itself. The peasantry would again be reluctant to deliver their farm produce in the absence of consumer goods, and agriculture would again decline. Foreseeing this, Stalin cast about for some way of insuring a supply of grain for the cities as well as for export in order to pay for needed industrial purchases from abroad.

His solution was forced collectivization. Since the peasants would not join the collectives voluntarily, they were compelled to—by party functionaries, the police and even the Army. The peasants were stubborn and at first resisted by the time-honored peasant method of refusing to sow or harvest. They buried their grain and slaughtered their livestock. The result was a ghastly famine in 1932 and 1933.

In 1933 visitors to the normally rich Kuban area found entire villages utterly deserted. In others a few old women, dazed with hunger, shuffled feebly around their burned-out huts or crawled about the harvested fields collecting chaff and munching it like famished animals.

IN spite of these calamities Stalin succeeded in enforcing the collectivization program, and by the mid-1930s agriculture in the Soviet Union was almost fully collectivized. The dictator had thus insured his food supply —at least for the time being.

Stalin had a second reason for pressing ahead with the collectivization program. Ever since the Revolution the food problem had been a favorite object of Bolshevik panaceas. Lenin's first proposed solution was the inauguration of a gigantic rural electrification program. But the new Soviet state did not have enough capital to finance it, and the program was never completed. Indeed, it had not been completed

even by 1965. In March of that year Leonid Brezhnev reported that 12 per cent of the collectives still had not been electrified. It was also suggested that the shortage of meat could be overcome by the mass breeding of rabbits. But the unpopularity of rabbit meat as an article of diet soon put an end to that dream. Eying the mechanized farms of the United States, Stalin proposed the organization of large farms that would be furnished with tractors. Mechanization, he believed, would make it possible for Russian agriculture to produce enough food to feed the population. At the same time it would release millions of peasants to work in the growing Soviet industrial centers.

Thousands of tractors were imported from the United States and Europe, and several factories were built to produce Soviet tractors. Machine Tractor Stations were set up throughout the countryside to cultivate and harvest the fields in return for payment in kind. Since the peasants were not given their share of the crop until both the Government and the tractor stations had received their share, drought or failure to harvest in time meant the loss of the peasants' portion.

But like Lenin's electrification scheme and the rabbit-breeding scheme, the mechanization program was a failure. The Soviet tractors were poorly designed and badly made, and Stalin refused to spend his foreign currency on the purchase of tractors from abroad. Spare parts were almost nonexistent and repair facilities were utterly inadequate. To this day, as Brezhnev has reported, it is not unusual for 40 per cent of the collective machinery to be out of repair at the peak of the season.

IF, when the Revolution occurred, the Bolsheviks had carried Marxism to its logical conclusion, they would immediately have organized all the agricultural land into state-run farms and paid the peasants regular salaries, like factory workers. Some state farms, or *sovkhoz*, were indeed organized on these principles. But this system had two drawbacks. It deprived the peasants of even the thinnest claim to the land Lenin had ostensibly given them. More important, in Stalin's eyes, equipping state farms with machinery demanded large capital investment at a time when all the resources of the state were being poured into heavy industry. Stalin was unwilling to make the investment in agriculture since this would have handicapped the industrialization program.

Later, however, when the pinch was less severe, the state farms multiplied. In 1963 they constituted 45 per cent of the total crop land. But in the early days the collectives were the major form of agricultural organization. The herds and tools, other than machinery, came from the members' original stocks, and all capital improvements, such as new buildings and equipment, were financed out of the collective profits. The collective farms therefore cost the state little or nothing. They even became a major source of revenue. The Government bought grain from the collectives very cheaply and then sold it to the consumers in the cities at exorbitant prices.

During the 1930s the misery on the farms was so great that millions fled to the cities to work in the new Soviet industries, and only women, children and old people were left to work the fields. This remnant was so apathetic that despite the efforts of party organizers and propagandists it was a constant problem to get them into the fields even at the height of the sowing or harvesting seasons. Even today women make up a large proportion of the Soviet farm labor force. The heavy casualty lists of World War II sharply reduced the number of men available for agricultural work.

STALIN made one concession to the peasants. He permitted each household to retain its private plot and a few livestock. These plots and the livestock soon became the peasants' chief source of food and cash. As a result the peasants gave much more attention to them than they did to the collective fields or herds. Whenever the peasants' bias became too obvious Stalin reduced the private

acreage and livestock holdings. But when food was scarce and supplies to the farm markets dried up, the private plots were again allowed to expand.

These last remnants of private property in the Soviet Union now constitute slightly more than 3 per cent of the total agricultural land. But they produce about a half of the gross agricultural output, including almost half of the livestock products.

Thanks in part to the private plots and in part to plain brute force, Stalin somehow managed throughout the '30s to get enough food from the collectives to feed his city workers—although they were on short rations. During World War II he maintained food production by relaxing the collective system and permitting the peasants to expand their private plots. In addition, he received help from abroad. The United States, acting under the Lend-Lease program, contributed large quanties of food for both military and civilian consumption. The American contribution was, however, only a small fraction of the total supply of food.

AFTER the war Stalin again tightened his grip on the farms. His harsh methods succeeded in raising yields and production sufficiently to provide an adequate supply of starchy foods for the expanding population. By 1948 it even became possible to abolish food rationing. But although the Soviet diet was adequate, it was anything but satisfactory. Meat, milk, butter and vegetables were constantly in short supply. These shortages continued until Stalin's death in 1953.

As in the case of industry, agricultural policy was drastically modified by Stalin's successors. Khrushchev, who was the son of a peasant, was the first Soviet leader with firsthand farm experience. He took a keen personal interest in agricultural problems—too personal, his successors later said.

His first reform was to raise the prices paid to peasants to provide an incentive for increasing production. His next was to decentralize agricultural planning and to consolidate many of the collectives into large units. By 1959 this had reduced the number of collectives from some 90,000 to fewer than 70,000. Moreover, instead of Moscow's dictating what crops were to be planted where, the local authorities were allowed to decide what crops to plant—provided always they delivered the quotas required by the state.

In a venturesome gamble Khrushchev ordered that the dry steppe land of central Siberia and Kazakhstan, the so-called Virgin Lands, be plowed up and sown to grain. Both Soviet and foreign agronomists warned him that he was risking the development of dust bowls like those that had blighted Canada and the United States in earlier years. But Khrushchev would not be deterred. If only three harvests out of five were successful, the entire cost of organizing, manning and equipping the venture would be recouped. In 1954 hundreds of thousands of young people were sent to the Asiatic steppes to set up state farms.

Finally, and even more dramatically, Khrushchev abolished the Machine Tractor Stations and sold their machines to the farms. With the machines went the drivers and mechanics. Now the farms were able to plan their own agricultural operations without interference from these powerful outside organizations.

The abolition of the tractor stations dissipated much of the power Stalin had built to control the peasantry. However, consolidation of the farms was accompanied by expansion of the party organizations on each farm, thus assuring Khrushchev the control he needed.

IN the first few years of his leadership Khrushchev's reforms paid off. In 1958 Khrushchev could boast of a record grain harvest. He even asserted that within a few years the Soviet Union would catch up with the United States in per capita production of meat, butter and milk. So confident was he of his innovations that he reduced capital investment in the farms from 11.3 per cent to 7.5 per cent of the national total. But in 1959 yields and total production fell off. Until then they had been increasing at an average of 7.6 per cent each year. Thereafter the increase fell off sharply to a mere 1.9 per cent. The increase in yields of basic crops dropped by 50 per cent. As Brezhnev later said, agriculture "in essence marked time."

As production still failed to rise sufficiently Khrushchev resorted to one expedient after another to increase the grain yield. He stepped up supervision of the collectives and divided the party apparatus into industrial and agricultural sectors to increase its supervision of the countryside. At one moment he denounced Government agencies for meddling in the farmers' affairs and in the next he scolded them for their lack of vigilance. Reorganizations of the

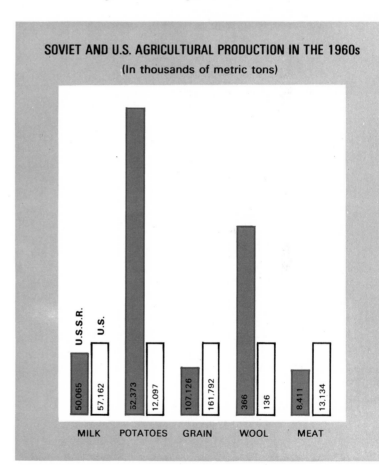

SOVIET AND U.S. AGRICULTURAL PRODUCTION IN THE 1960s

(In thousands of metric tons)

U.S.S.R. | U.S.

MILK — 50,065 | 57,162
POTATOES — 52,373 | 12,097
GRAIN — 107,126 | 161,792
WOOL — 366 | 136
MEAT — 8,411 | 13,134

AGRICULTURAL OUTPUT of the Soviet Union and the United States in some selected commodities is shown on the chart above. A per capita breakdown would show greater productivity for the U.S. In 1962, for instance, U.S. meat production was estimated at 189.6 pounds per person, as against 73.4 pounds in the Soviet Union.

state and party farm administration followed each other in rapid succession.

Despite everything, however, farm production still did not increase at the rate Khrushchev had promised. Droughts in the Virgin Lands produced wind erosion, and concentration on sowing only wheat produced a scourge of weeds sometimes called "the green fire."

In a frantic attempt to increase the sown area Khrushchev ordered that crop rotation be stopped and that meadows and pastures be plowed up. But production still failed to rise enough. Then in 1963 a severe drought sharply reduced the harvest. Rationing was reintroduced and the Soviets were compelled to buy huge quantities of grain abroad.

In the summer of 1964, apparently panicked by his successive failures, Khrushchev proposed still another panacea. For the first time, he dealt with the heart of the agricultural problem —the collective system itself. Collective farmers, he suggested, should be assigned specific fields to cultivate and should be reimbursed according to the amount they produced. The similarity of this proposed innovation to private "capitalist" farming and the retreat from the collective principle was too obvious to escape the notice of the more orthodox of his colleagues. Khrushchev was ousted before he could institute his latest reform.

His successors were quick to point out his mistakes. Vladimir Matskevich, an able man whom Khrushchev had dismissed from his position as National Minister of Agriculture, was returned to the post. His comment on his former master's methods was bitter. They were, he said, "irrational schemes . . . that were supposed to work miracles."

WITH Khrushchev's ouster many of his reforms were rescinded. The division of the party into urban and rural sectors was abolished. Scientific methods of cultivation were reintroduced. The "miracle crops" were curtailed. Under Khrushchev the prices of farm products, especially livestock, had sometimes been lower than the cost of production. Now they were substantially raised. To assure the farmers that demands on their production would not be subject to whimsical fluctuations, Brezhnev established an annual delivery quota well under Khrushchev's and promised that it would not be altered for at least five years. In addition he pledged to invest $78.8 billion in the farms and their equipment in the next five years—a sum as great as had been invested in the previous 19 years. The expenditures would be primarily for new buildings, new irrigation projects, the manufacture of new farm machinery—with special emphasis on spare parts— and, above all, an adequate supply of fertilizers.

IN some ways Brezhnev's reforms sounded oddly reminiscent of earlier ones that had died a-borning. But agricultural specialists hailed the new program. It was, they said, the frankest admission of the problems of Soviet agriculture ever published, and the reforms, they insisted, were the most realistic yet proposed. But the question remained whether Brezhnev would keep his promises, since they might necessitate the sacrifice of badly needed industrial and defense resources.

Basically the new leaders promised the farmers a fairer deal—a fairer share of capital investments and a fairer monetary return for their labors. But one fundamental aspect of the problem was scarcely mentioned. It was all very well to promise the peasant a higher income. But how was he going to spend it? To provide consumer goods in sufficient quantity and adequate quality for the rural population would require a major expansion of consumer industries in the cities.

Once again the Kremlin leaders were faced with their most acute dilemma: the allocation of resources. Were they prepared to discard the fetish of heavy-industry priority and pare down investments in arms, space and related industries? Would they finally prepare to devote an adequate share of the country's capital resources to the consumer, particularly the rural consumer, the mistrusted peasant whose needs had been ignored for generations?

*On a farm near Alma-Ata a peasant gathers hay, using one of the primitive methods that are gradually vanishing from the U.S.S.R.*

# Struggle to Produce More Food

The desperate attempt of the Kremlin over the past decade to increase the Soviet Union's agricultural yield has taken place in a land that is in large part poor for crops. While some areas are ideal for growing a wide variety of grains and other produce, others are only marginally useful and a great many are unfit for cultivation. This disparity, combined with the poor climatic conditions that exist in many regions, has given added drama to the Kremlin's relentless drive to mechanize Soviet farms and to organize the country's peasants for greater production.

**SWEEPING WHEAT** that has just come from modern combines, teen-age girls on a collective near the Kazakhstan border use primitive twig brooms (*above*) to pile up the grain for cleaning. Later the grain will be dried and then stored. In recent years there has been a trend toward reorganizing such farms into ever larger economic units.

*A farm village in Siberia is laid out on characteristic collective lines. Peasants can grow crops for themselves on plots just behind their*

BAKING BREAD, a woman on the Vazisubani Collective in Georgia prepares the traditional flat, unleavened loaves for her family (*above*). The coal oven is in her backyard.

*houses, but all of the large fields beyond are collectively owned.*

FOLK DANCING, a Georgian girl, Violetta Sakhvadze, flirts with her partner (*above*) at a carefree party held on Georgia's Rustaveli Collective. Violetta is a tea picker.

**GEORGIAN COWBOYS** drive cattle through a gravel stream bed (*above*) on their way to pasture in the Caucasus Mountains, where the cowboys will live for three months.

**CENTRAL ASIAN COTTON PICKERS** load a wagon in a new cotton-producing part of the Fergana Valley (*opposite*). Most of the U.S.S.R.'s cotton comes from Central Asia.

**STATE TEA PICKERS**, women laborers who are paid a salary by the Government, work (*above*) on the Salingikh State Farm, one of the largest agricultural units in Georgia.

**ESTONIAN FISHERMEN** unload their catch of sprats (*right*) on the dock of the Kirov Fishery Collective near Tallinn. The Soviet fish catch rose 60 per cent from 1958 to 1963.

**FARM MECHANIZATION** *is gradually increasing. Major field work is performed by machines, but much processing work is done by hand*

**SPRAY RIG,** mounted on a tractor (*above*), is the pride of the men and women who work on the big Vazisubani Collective, located in Georgia. The rig evenly covers both sides of two rows of grapevines with an insecticide.

**MANUAL LABOR** is carried out by women (*left*) on a collective farm in Irkutsk, Siberia. Siberian agriculture is also becoming mechanized, however, and the Government is trying to convert more of its people to farming.

**GRASS MIXER** is fed by women farm workers (*opposite*) on the Dzhenashar Collective in Kazakhstan. The machine chops the grass into fine particles and blends in egg whites and vitamins to make a special cattle feed.

FOOD DISTRIBUTION *is only slowly being modernized.*
*Consumers can usually buy nothing but perishables*
*grown locally, since refrigerated transportation is scarce*

**IN A GEORGIAN MARKET** in Tbilisi men and women from collective farms sell grapes. The rich wines of mountainous Georgia are highly prized throughout Russia.

**SHOPPING FOR VEGETABLES** in a Moscow free market, a girl buys cabbage. Farmers from the Moscow area bring surplus produce here and charge what the traffic will bear.

PROSPERING FARMER, Ivan
Teslenko joins his wife in
readying an evening meal in
their home near Kiev. Teslenko holds the position of
chairman of their collective.

# 6

# Classes in a Classless Society

DESPITE Marx's promises of a classless so-ciety, and despite the Bolshevik liquida-tion first of the Russian aristocracy, then of the bourgeoisie and finally of the successful small farmers, or kulaks, class distinctions in the So-viet Union are becoming more marked with each passing year.

Marx and his disciples believed that class lines were based on the ownership of the means of production. If private ownership could be done away with, classes would disappear. But as Mi-lovan Djilas of Yugoslavia, possessor of one of the sharpest minds and most courageous wills in the Communist world, has pointed out, it is not ownership of production that counts, but control. Like the managers of American in-dustry today, Communist Party officials do not own their plants but they exercise control over the economy, and with control and the im-portance of the functions a man executes in

## Classes in a Classless Society

Soviet society come the perquisites and privileges on which modern classes are founded. As a result of these perquisites and privileges the new upper classes of the Soviet Union are able to pass on to their children their accumulated wealth, cultural tastes, intellectual aspirations and educational opportunities and thereby help perpetuate their class.

IN its present stage of development Soviet society is still more flexible than many of the older societies of Western Europe. The average young Russian today has many opportunities to rise from humble origins, perhaps more than his counterpart does in any other modern nation except the United States. But the opportunities of climbing up the Soviet ladder—and the chances of falling down it— are steadily diminishing.

Because of the reticence of Soviet statisticians, it is almost impossible to draw precise lines between classes on the basis of income. To attempt to do so, in fact, is to betray one's Western or, at least, non-Marxist orientation; in Soviet society position and privilege have nothing to do with income. Income increases the higher a citizen climbs in the hierarchy, of course, but increasing income cannot buy larger apartments in Moscow, *dachas* in its environs or vacations on the Black Sea. Such rewards are granted on the basis of the functions the citizen carries out for the state. The more highly the state values his functions, the higher the privileges.

It is possible, however, to examine cases in each of the major categories into which Soviet society seems to break down. In one of the recently completed apartment houses in Moscow lives a couple we shall call Yuri and Lydia. Their apartment consists of only two rooms and a bath and it is cramped and uncomfortable, but it contrasts favorably with the barrack they lived in until a few years ago, when it was torn down to provide room for the new housing. There they shared an outhouse with other families and had to walk outdoors across slippery planks laid in a sea of

mud to obtain water from the spigot that supplied all the families who lived in the barrack.

In the daytime the apartment house is empty, for the men and women are at work and the children are at school or in a nursery. Around 7 p.m. Lydia returns from the cafeteria in which she works as a waitress, bringing her two-year-old, whom she has picked up at a state-run nursery. Half an hour later Yuri, an unskilled construction worker, trudges home. He brings with him a small parcel containing some bread and sausage and a bottle filled with milk. He had taken the bottle to work in the morning and had it filled after work.

Leaving the child with Yuri, Lydia makes her way to the kitchen that the family shares with another family and prepares some milk and grits for the child.

When the meal is ready she feeds the baby and puts him to bed in the rear room. Then she and Yuri eat a cold supper of bread, sausage and tea. The meal is not a large one for both have had a hot midday meal at their places of work.

Occasionally, Yuri and Lydia treat themselves to a movie, but otherwise their recreation is confined to visiting friends, attending the free jazz or classical music concerts in the Gorki Park of Culture and Rest, or window-shopping on Sundays and holidays.

YURI earns 80 rubles—a little more than $80—a month, and Lydia makes about $50 a month. The two wages add up to $135 a month, about the minimum on which a family of three can live—which is one reason why so many women work in the Soviet Union. Out of their monthly income they spend about $100 for food: a pound or two of beef every week, bread, margarine, tea, potatoes, a few vegetables, milk and sugar.

Almost all the rest of the family income is spent on clothing, and not very much of it at that because shirts sell for $6, suits for $110, shoes for $23 and rayon dresses for $29. As a consequence both Yuri and Lydia wear light, inexpensive sandals in summer and rubber boots in winter. Each of them has a shabby overcoat, but the baby has a heavy imitation fur coat and fur hat. Yuri and Lydia feel, as do most Russian parents, that the children come first.

Rent is only a few dollars a month for Yuri and Lydia. The charge, based on a few cents per square yard per month, presents no problem inasmuch as the whole family occupies only a few square yards. Medical bills are also no problem because doctors' services and hospital care are free. There is a small charge, however, for eyeglasses and drugs. Almost all of the drugs available in the West are also produced in Russia. The common ones, from aspirin to streptomycin, are generally available; the newest and more exotic are in short supply and difficult to obtain.

Soviet medical students say privately that the frequent mental disorders among poorer people are brought about largely by overcrowding and lack of privacy. Lack of good housing has also been named as a factor in the low Russian birth rate.

Perhaps the most prevalent "disease" among the working class, however, is sheer boredom, and the commonest medicine for this is vodka. A half-liter bottle (midway between a pint and a fifth) sells for about three dollars. Most Russians, regardless of class or income, somehow manage to find the money for it.

Soviet statistics give no indication of the size of this lowest class. It may be taken to include all those people who earn less than $100 a month, which is the average wage of urban workers in the U.S.S.R. today. But it has been estimated that more than half of the entire Soviet population is in this wage bracket.

HOW do Yuri and Lydia reconcile their situation with the Communist regime's long-standing promises of paradise? Few if any of the lowest class are members of the party or even of Komsomol, for if they were they would long since have acquired better quarters and better jobs. Yuri's schooling is finished, and because only a better education could assure him of substantial future advancement he

has little hope of rising appreciably above his present level.

Yuri and Lydia both recognize, however, that living conditions have been improving perceptibly in the past few years. With enough to eat, they already have something to lose, and though they grumble over their lot and have no love for the regime, their minds are preoccupied with the problems of daily living.

Furthermore, as Russian citizens they have a strong feeling of reverence for and pride in their country, and though they may resent the priority of spaceships over shoes they derive some solace from their association with Soviet technological and scientific accomplishments. Toward the regime itself their reaction is principally one of apathy and resignation, tempered with the self-abasement reflected in the ancient peasant saying: "We are a dark people."

IN another district of Moscow the attention of a passerby is attracted by the sound of singing that emerges from the lighted windows of a different apartment house, a modern-looking building of five stories. It is the evening of November 7, the Soviet national holiday. In the apartment a table is set for the great annual holiday dinner of cold ham, sardines, margarine, bread, cheese, cucumber and potato salad. A small, half-empty carafe of vodka sits on the table, together with a bottle of sweet red wine. On a kerosene stove in the corner a can of goulash is warming, and its strong smell permeates the room. Two couples are seated around the table, and in one of the two bedrooms two small children are asleep. The apartment has a modern kitchen and bath, walk-in closets and a balcony.

In low voices the two couples are singing an old Russian song that is as deep and mournful as a dirge. Their faces are as solemn and as sad as the song. At the end of the song the men pour themselves some vodka, the women some wine. They toast one another gravely, take a bite of food and sing again.

The occupants of this apartment are one rung up the ladder from Yuri and Lydia. The host, whom we may call Stepan, is a Government clerk and makes up to $120 a month. His wife Natasha is a secretary and earns $80 a month. The relatively expensive banquet laid out on the table before them does not reflect these salaries, for the Russian's pride and sense of hospitality dictate that when he celebrates he must turn his pockets inside out and leave them empty until the next payday comes along.

Stepan and others like him—foremen, technicians and skilled workers who are paid between $100 and $250 a month—represent perhaps 30 to 40 per cent of the urban wage earners of the Soviet Union. In a way Stepan and Natasha are better off than many others in their income bracket, for they live in Moscow, only a stone's throw from the Kremlin, the center of their universe.

Stepan and Natasha also lived in different quarters until a few years ago. They had a single room, one of four in a basement apartment. Each of the other rooms was occupied by a family like theirs, and all of the families shared a tiny kitchen that supplemented the kerosene stoves they kept in their rooms. A single bathroom and a single toilet served a dozen people. In 1963, however, Stepan and Natasha were allocated one of the city's new apartments. When selected, they hurried to the unfurnished house, picked their own wallpapers and paints, and managed to find the money to buy some new furniture.

They are not necessarily permanent residents of the new apartment. When, as sometimes happens, disputes break out among the tenants in Moscow apartments, order is to be restored by the house manager, a glorified janitor who may serve four or five apartment houses with perhaps a thousand tenants. If he fails, an extralegal "Comradely Court," composed of tenants selected by the building's senior party members, can put the offenders on trial. The court can levy minor fines or it can even recommend to the police that the troublemakers' residence permits for Moscow—perhaps their most precious privilege—be rescinded, forcing them to move to the provinces.

In addition to the children, families in these apartments often include grandparents, who can serve as baby-sitters and can spend their free hours standing in line to buy scarce items. Because space is limited the grandparents frequently must share a room with the children.

Like Yuri and Lydia, Stepan and Natasha allot the major share of their family budget to food. They do have a little more left over for clothes, but they have very little for entertainment. The guests they are entertaining are a young doctor and his wife, who because of the husband's professional status are considered to be members of the Soviet intelligentsia. But as the doctor looks critically at his shabby suit he complains to Natasha, "How can anyone belong to the intelligentsia in a suit like this? And how can one have anything better on a salary of only a hundred and twenty dollars a month?"

Occasionally Stepan and Natasha can afford a movie or even the theater but generally they spend their evenings in their apartment reading. Russians are voracious readers and it does not cost much to get a book from one of the numerous bookstores.

Books by Western authors are very popular and are approved by the Government if they reflect discredit on the capitalist system. Social protest works, either from the darkest days of the Industrial Revolution or the Depression of the 1930s, constitute the staple, with no reference to the fact that anything has changed for

---

**A RUSSIAN BUDGET**

Monthly expenses for Stepan and Natasha are shown on the list below. Durable goods include house supplies. The income tax was supposed to disappear by 1965, but it continues to be levied on all but the lowest-income groups.

| | |
|---|---|
| Food | $100 |
| Clothing | 40 |
| Rent and utilities | 8 |
| Recreation, durable goods | 25 |
| Income tax | 12 |
| Miscellaneous | 15 |
| Total | $200 |

---

the better in the West since those days. John Steinbeck's *The Grapes of Wrath* and Sinclair Lewis' *Babbitt* are well known, although Ernest Hemingway remains the all-time favorite author. Western science and adventure fiction are extremely popular; Ray Bradbury (*The Martian Chronicles, Fahrenheit 451*) is devoured. Mark Twain is revered, as is Jack London, who is considered to be perhaps the greatest American author. William Faulkner and J. D. Salinger are highly rated by the intelligentsia. John Updike has recently gained acclaim for his novel *The Centaur*. Arthur Miller's plays are also widely read.

Even though their life and surroundings appear somewhat drab by American standards, Stepan and Natasha will tell you that things are better than ever before. In contrast to the situation a few years ago the stores of Moscow today are full of things to buy. Many of these things are as yet too expensive for their means, but they now have a television set and they look forward to one day acquiring some of the gadgets in the dream kitchen that Natasha saw at the 1959 American Exhibition in Moscow.

But what encourages people like them who have not yet been assigned to the new apartments are the acres of new housing springing up in the suburbs. The lack of adequate housing has long evoked the Russian people's bitterest complaints, not merely in Moscow and other big cities but in the smaller provincial towns and new industrial communities back of the Urals, where for many years people have occupied space scarcely larger than the beds they sleep in.

RUSSIA'S housing shortage was not acute until the 1930s. In the early years of the Communist regime many city dwellers had gone back to the villages in search of food. But when Stalin started his industrial drive in 1929 the cities were flooded with new workers. Moscow's population grew from a million and a half to five million in a single generation.

Although Stalin did put up some buildings in the larger cities, this did not begin to provide adequate space for the new workers. The crowding became so severe that after Stalin's death his successors quickly sought a remedy.

The first post-Stalin attempts were only half-hearted, and they bogged down in the general shortage of housing materials brought about by the priority given to heavy industry. Not until Khrushchev turned to the problem in 1956 was any real headway made. Ordering an end to all fanciful architectural designs, Khrushchev instructed his engineers to devise techniques for mass housing production. Today great square, gray blocks of apartment buildings made of concrete slabs are mushrooming in all large Soviet cities just as quickly as the cement can be made and the slabs poured.

The buildings themselves often have the defects implicit in hasty construction. Door handles come off in one's hands, windows fail to close, electric wiring is faulty, floors buckle and walls crack a few weeks after they are finished.

YET for all these defects the new buildings represent the height of ambition for the tenants of the ancient, crowded buildings where most urban dwellers live today. For regardless of their shoddy construction they provide what Russians today long for more than anything else: privacy.

The lack of privacy has been blamed not only for the low birth rate and the increase in nervous disorders but also for the high Soviet divorce rate. Jammed into cramped quarters, families have jangled each other's nerves to such an extent that children have left their parents and the parents have left each other.

The longing for a measure of privacy is nowhere more apparent than in the communities of private houses that began to sprout on the outskirts of most of the smaller cities of Russia a few years ago. When Khrushchev launched his housing drive, he encouraged city councils to allocate plots to private home builders and ordered industry to provide the necessary building materials. In many towns the response was so great that private housing was soon going up almost as fast as Government-sponsored apartments. And the first thing most of the private builders put up was a high wooden fence around their plot.

The private housing program has been de-emphasized in recent years, although a family can still get some land and can arrange financial matters to buy material for a house. But the program is not being pushed, and the procedure is somewhat more arduous than it used to be. In the larger cities, cooperatives are really the coming thing. No hard figures are obtainable, but it has been reported that cooperatives now constitute 70 per cent of all new apartments. Several sources agree that the percentage is certainly more than half. Most middle-class families can afford the down payment with little strain. By doing so they can obtain an apartment faster, in a slightly better building, and know that in the future they will have a say in how it is maintained. That is a crucial factor. The apartment owners can vote to have the hallways painted or to hire a night lobby guard and know that the work will be done because it is they who will pay. In rental apartment buildings, getting maintenance work done is a tremendous problem. Since the same workers and engineers build both the cooperatives and the public housing, there is little difference in the standards of construction. The prefabricated concrete-panel type of construction that has been pushed to replace brick is plagued with problems, and tenants much prefer the brick. Finishing work in the cooperatives, as in the public housing, is poor.

JUST across the river from the Kremlin, by the Stone Bridge, rises a large concrete apartment building in the severe style of the late 1920s. Once a light gray, the porous cement of which it was made has absorbed three decades of Moscow soot and is now an ugly black, unwashable and unpaintable, a dreary reminder of Stalin's one excursion into functional architecture. It was long known as the Dom Pravitelstva, the House of the Government. It was built to house the favored members of the Communist hierarchy after Stalin,

denouncing egalitarianism, had declared that high officials should enjoy the comforts commensurate with their station.

The tenants of the Dom once included such prominent men as Nikolai Bukharin, the last of Stalin's major rivals to be killed; Karl Radek, the propagandist who is presumed to have died after many years of exile in eastern Siberia; and a dozen other Old Bolsheviks. Its current tenants, however, feel more secure in their occupancy. Although many of the newer apartment houses are more luxurious and spacious, and many of the elite have dispersed to them, the Dom is still the original homestead of the upper middle class.

Its apartments are multiroomed and usually occupied not by a small tribe of children, grandparents and country cousins but by the immediate family of a successful writer, artist or party functionary. Some of the apartments are penthouses, while others boast large balconies overlooking the Kremlin and the Moskva River. Most have a full complement of servants —cooks, maids and nursemaids.

THE contemporary Soviet elite consists of top industrial managers and plant directors, leading engineers, senior military officers, popular novelists and artists, university professors and members of the Academy of Sciences. In this class, incomes vary between $5,000 and $10,000 a year and can go as high as $25,000. In purchasing power such incomes are worth considerably more than they would be in America. All together, these members of the elite probably comprise less than 15 per cent of the country's population.

Most of the members of this group maintain *dachas* and many actually own them. The *dacha* is a peculiarly Russian institution that reflects the strong attachment of almost every Russian to the soil, the forest and nature. Probably millions of city dwellers go each summer "to the *dacha.*" It may be a room just big enough for a bed in a tumble-down shack, or it may be a large masonry villa complete with billiard room and solarium and situated in a

100

wooded park, with a boathouse and a speedboat on a lake or the Moskva River. Owners of these sumptuous villas, if they do not own a car, may have the use of a chauffeur-driven car from the plant or institute at which they work.

Many of them also take vacations on the Black Sea coast, where, if they do not have a villa of their own, they take de luxe accommodations at the better hotels and sanatoriums along the coast.

Because they hold influential positions in the party, on the production side of the economy or in other areas of great importance to the state, many of them live better than their salaries would indicate. Among the benefits they enjoy is the opportunity to accept goods and services in exchange for the political favors that they can dispense.

FOR the most part risen from modest surroundings, the members of the upper middle class in Russia have a passion for culture. These are the people who fill the thirty-odd theaters of Moscow and the hundreds of provincial theaters and opera houses every night of the week. They compete with each other in buying whatever modern paintings the young artists produce, and some spend huge sums buying what few relics of the old aristocracy are still left in the antique shops of Moscow and Leningrad: Meissen china, jewelry, Fabergé enamels and porcelain Easter eggs.

Much of their income goes to their wardrobes, for like the newly rich everywhere they are painfully self-conscious of their appearance. They will spend half a month's salary to buy a few yards of French dress material or English suiting on a trip abroad or to purchase such material at GUM, a big department store on Red Square. They will spend another half having the material made into a dress or suit by one of the few good tailors in town.

But probably their most serious concern is their children. Many of them started life as manual workers, and they abhor the thought that their children may have to work again as laborers. Knowing that a university education is the only road to jobs as good as theirs, they go to great lengths to assure their children's entrance into the crowded universities. Often they employ private tutors to prepare their sons for the stiff entrance examinations. Occasionally they resort to pressure or even outright bribery of college officials in order to have their children enrolled.

A SMALL minority among the adults of this class may dream of an increase in spiritual rather than material rewards and may long for such imponderables as increased freedom of self-expression, but the concern of the majority is to avoid rocking the boat that has brought them to such affluence. In sharp contrast to the dedicated older party leaders who originally conquered Russia for Communism, the upper middle class is bent on keeping things as they are and avoiding adventures both at home and abroad.

On the right bank of the Moskva River in southwest Moscow, in an area once known as Sparrow Hills and now Lenin Hills, are five stately white mansions. Across the river is the Luzhniki Sports Park, and beyond it are the towers of the Kremlin. Each of the mansions stands on a large plot surrounded by a high fence. Ordinarily a uniformed policeman can be seen patrolling the sidewalk.

Just who it is that occupies these houses at any given moment is a constant source of speculation to politically minded Muscovites. But there is no doubt what group the occupants represent. They are men at the pinnacle of the Soviet regime: high-ranking members of the party Presidium or the Council of Ministers.

The salary of a Soviet leader is not public knowledge, and it is not very important. In the early days after the Revolution the party leaders deliberately limited their incomes to relatively low amounts. But since these leaders are supplied with cars and chauffeurs, probably with household staffs and certainly with special housing, their cash salaries are secondary.

Furthermore most of them receive very large sums from the publication of their "literary works." These are often no more than collections of their speeches, but they are published in editions of hundreds of thousands of copies and are required reading for the party membership. Royalties from such editions can run to extremely high figures.

SHARING the privileged status of the party leaders and Government ministers—though not their power—are a handful of senior scientists, writers, artists and generals, many of whom are highly paid. Together they comprise only a fraction of 1 per cent of the population. They are the cream of the cream.

In addition to their apartments in Moscow and their luxuriously appointed *dachas*—occasionally a single family has several—many of this top group also maintain sumptuous villas on the Black Sea. Stalin used to reward leading personalities by giving them a seaside house, often one suddenly vacated when the dictator liquidated its owner. But now these villas have been confiscated and are allocated to Government or party leaders for temporary use according to their political importance.

Since the war a favorite resort for the very wealthy has been Karlovy Vary (formerly Carlsbad) in Czechoslovakia. Before World War II many of the most prominent of Europe's aristocracy went there to "take the cure." Today, where once kings and emperors congregated, top Soviet actors, dancers and writers bask in new-found luxury.

Membership in this group today is as exclusive as high society in Western capitals has ever been. The luxurious standard of living and high connections of its members tend to keep them aloof from even the rich managers and professors of the upper middle class. Occasionally they may take in a rising young engineer much as the smart set of London or New York might adopt and lionize a young poet. But generally they keep to themselves, even to the extent of marrying within the confines of the group.

Income taxes have never been higher than 13 per cent in Soviet Russia, so the members of the elite can look forward to keeping most of their money. Though Marx inveighed against inherited wealth, there is no inheritance tax in the Soviet Union beyond a simple probate fee. Thus the very rich can guarantee that their children will also be rich.

*Dacha* parties, dancing and record-collecting are the chief preoccupations of the younger members of the group, although all of them are required to safeguard their status as "useful citizens" by enrolling in some educational institute. From time to time the debauchery and orgies of these younger people, who are known as "golden youth," lead to crimes and scandals. But these seldom reach the pages of the country's press.

THE stratification of Russia's society into classes has never been part of the Kremlin's plan for building socialism. On the contrary, it has taken place as the unavoidable consequence of a society's rising from poverty and want, and it has occurred, at least in the upper strata, against the better judgment of old Communists who have always sought the classless society.

One reason it has taken place is that, more than in any Western country, children in Russia occupy the place of privilege. Even the poorest parent tends to lavish what small possessions he has on his sons and daughters. And in the upper classes the determination of parents to give their children the advantages they as children of the Revolution were denied has been stronger than any Kremlin decree that has been thus far promulgated.

The political effect that the hardening of class lines is having upon the ideological purity of the Soviet state is of deep concern to the party leaders—even though their own families are among the most prominent beneficiaries of the development. More than once the Kremlin leaders have warned that the desire for higher living standards must not diminish the national effort to expand Soviet and Communist power. But there seems to be no stopping the formation of classes in a classless society.

*Alexander Lozovan, a civil engineer (right), his son and wife listen to daughter Natasha at the piano in their Moscow apartment.*

# New Affluence for a Rising Middle Class

In certain areas, life in the Soviet Union has come to resemble life in the West. Many families have not yet achieved the comfortable middle-class status of the Alexander Lozovans (*above and on the next two pages*), but most Russians now at least look on the Lozovans' position as an achievable goal. With the availability of more consumer goods and more and better housing—plus such occasional frills as Western-style night life—some of the country's bleakness and austerity is slowly being alleviated.

# A PROSPEROUS FAMILY, *the*
## *Lozovans live in a new apartment with up-to-date luxuries*

**AT THE OFFICE,** Alexander Lozovan, 51, gives orders by telephone (*above*) to a construction crew working on a new residential district of Moscow called Medvedkovo.

**UNDER THE DRIER,** Lozovan's wife, Eliena, 38 (*above, far right*), keeps an appointment. Referring to their life over 10 years, she says, "Oh, God, don't let it go back."

**BEFORE EXAMS,** the Lozovans' son Sasha (*above*) studies for admission to the Moscow Higher Technical School. He passed and began an electrical engineering course.

**ON VACATION,** Natasha Lozovan (*below, center*), a music student, is interrupted by her mother and a friend at her paternal grandparents' home in the Ukraine.

**IN AFTERNOON SUN,** Anna Klugman, Mrs. Lozovan's mother, is silhouetted in their 12-by-18-foot living room (*above*). The apartment has two bedrooms, a kitchen with a new refrigerator, and a bathroom.

**AT MEALTIME,** Mrs. Lozovan (*left*) receives assistance from a friend. The Lozovans keep an extra bed for guests and a 12-inch television set in the kitchen. A magnifying glass is placed in front of the screen.

**IMAGINATIVE CAFE**, located at Baku, on the Caspian Sea, adds a light touch (*above*) to an oil-producing region. Such strikingly modern architectural styles, once rare, can now be seen in various regions of the Soviet Union.

**BALLROOM DANCING** is featured at the modern Neva Restaurant in Leningrad, most Westernized and cosmopolitan of Russian cities. The Soviet Union's night life, centering around restaurants, has expanded in recent years.

A WESTERN STYLE *becomes increasingly discernible in new manners and modes of the once-spare Communist world*

**LATEST FASHIONS** are put on display in Moscow by the popular designer Vyacheslav Mikhailovich Zaitsev and three of his models (*above*). Zaitsev's work is an innovation: most Soviet women dress like the one at right.

**ADDING A STORY** to a vast new suburban development outside Moscow, workmen put together factory-made units, a technique for fast, if not esthetic, building.

**ATTACHING WALLS,** masons apply cement (*left*). After years of cramped living, the Soviet Union is currently undertaking numerous crash housing programs.

**HOISTING A UNIT,** a crane moves a complete living room into place (*right*). Even bathrooms are fully outfitted when trucked from the factory to the apartment site.

## PREFABRICATED APARTMENTS *are changing city skylines as billions of rubles are spent on alleviating housing shortages*

**ENJOYING THE VIEW** from their apartment in the prefabricated development, Elena Zharinov and her daughters take their first look from their new balcony (*above*).

**INSPECTING A CLOSET**, Svetlana Zharinov explores a part of her new home (*below*). Apartments in the housing project feature several similar storage facilities.

IN SCIENCE CLASS at a Leningrad primary school a boy and a girl work with a microscope. The state spends large sums to equip the schools with the best teaching aids.

# 7

# The Schooling of Soviet Thought

NEAR the entrance to the Park of Culture and Rest in Dyushambe, in a far corner of the Soviet Union, a young man is standing on a small wooden platform. Before him a dozen or so strollers have stopped to listen, but most of the people glance at him and move on to watch a team of high-wire acrobats or to listen to a jazz band in a little outdoor theater.

The young man—blond, good-looking and obviously from European Russia—is speaking vigorously and well, expounding the current party position on international events. When he pauses for a moment an onlooker asks a question, and the speaker patiently answers it. Another question follows and again the young man gives the official answer.

The young man is a representative of one of the special Communist Party committees responsible for guiding public opinion in the Soviet Union. One widespread misconception about Russia is that public opinion plays no role in the Kremlin's political calculations. On the contrary, the Russian leaders pay as much attention to what their people are thinking as a wise military leader pays to the morale of his troops. For while public opinion in the Soviet Union, like morale in an army, does not guide Government policies or spark initiative as it sometimes does in the West, it does determine the degree of enthusiasm with which the population performs the tasks assigned to it and the degree of acquiescence with which it accepts the Kremlin's policies.

The man in the park is both a speaker and a pollster. When he returns to party headquarters he will prepare a detailed report on the frame of mind of his listeners, the questions they ask and their reactions to his answers—anything that will help his superiors gauge the state of public opinion at the moment.

AS the Communists began to consolidate their control after 1917, they recognized that to preserve themselves in power they would have to do more than propagate the party line to the masses. They would also have to prevent anyone else from spreading a different view. From the start they closely supervised all public communication. They screened and increasingly prohibited foreign newspapers, books and movies, and at the same time censored all publications within the country. In Stalin's later days nearly all public communication with the outside world was stopped, and after World War II great effort was made to prevent foreign broadcasts from reaching the Russian people.

Stalin's successors have relaxed many of these measures and have permitted contact with the outside world through tourism, cultural- and scientific-exchange programs, and such Russian language radio programs as those broadcast by the British Broadcasting Company and the Voice of America. But even today political ideas not consonant with Communist doctrine are suppressed.

The ultimate aim of the Soviet propaganda effort is to develop the New Soviet Man: the hero of socialism, free of all capitalist or bourgeois "prejudices," who will happily and unselfishly produce according to his abilities and consume according to his needs. This is also one of the principal goals of Soviet education. Both Lenin and Stalin recognized that the first prerequisite for a politically sound public state of mind was education. Before the Revolution 65 per cent of all Russia's citizens had been illiterate, and one of the first campaigns launched by the Bolsheviks was "the battle to stamp out illiteracy." The drive was remarkably successful: today illiteracy is almost nonexistent in the U.S.S.R.

STALIN had another compelling reason for improving public education. If he was to realize his hopes of making Russia into a modern industrial nation, he could not depend on foreign technicians indefinitely but would have to develop his own pool of experts. Schools and universities were organized not to produce well-educated men and women but to turn out engineers to build and operate the economy. Today they graduate a far higher proportion of engineers than does the United States.

Except for the children of very highly placed citizens, every young Russian knows that his entire future depends on his education. This education begins on an informal level, and very early. Nurseries care for the children of working parents from the time they are 10 weeks old until they are three. Thereafter the youngsters attend kindergarten until they are seven, when they begin the required eight years of primary school. Anyone who stops his education at the end of the required eight years knows that he will never rise above the ranks of unskilled labor. The 10-year-school graduate may rise another rung. The technical-school graduate rises farther, but unless he possesses a university diploma he can never get to the top of the ladder no matter how hard he works or how able he is. Thus with rare exceptions the Soviet self-made man is made in school and at the universities. Education has always been held in high esteem in Russia, and the Soviet need for trained personnel has enhanced its position of honor. Only the most hopeless students leave the eight-year schools before they have been graduated, and even these are sent to trade schools to complete the required program.

### WHO GOES TO SCHOOL

| | U.S.S.R. | U.S. |
|---|---|---|
| **SCHOOL ATTENDANCE: CHILDREN** | | |
| Preschool | 3,627,000 | 2,450,345 |
| Primary level | 31,300,000 | 27,697,406 |
| Secondary and technical-school level | 6,769,700 | 14,288,733 |
| Higher educational institutions | 2,639,900 | 3,726,114 |
| | | |
| **SCHOOL COMPLETION** | | |
| Completed primary level | 43,300,000 | 20,523,000 |
| Completed secondary level | 21,600,000 | 38,679,000 |
| Graduated from higher institutions | 7,500,000 | 10,163,000 |

EDUCATIONAL LEVEL of the Soviet people is compared to that in the United States. The figures for both nations are estimates. Despite its smaller population, the United States has more students in institutions on both the secondary- and the higher-education levels. Many Soviet men and women take correspondence courses, and the figure for the Soviet secondary and technical levels includes the students enrolled in such programs.

From first grade through the university level, tuition today is free. Most university students receive living allowances or stipends according to their academic standing and the subjects they are studying. Stipends are raised when it is necessary to attract students into certain professions and lowered to discourage entrance into nonessential professions. The number permitted to study for a given profession is determined by official estimates of the number of graduates the profession will need.

As a result students in Soviet universities do not have the free choice of future careers that Americans have. Many young men and women, for example, hope to go into journalism, perhaps because they believe it will give them an opportunity to travel and see the world. But the need for journalists is limited. Hence stipends for journalism students are low and vacancies in journalism courses few. But stipends and vacancies for mining students are high because the mining profession has been in need of skilled engineers for many years.

Four years of primary school was made obligatory for all children soon after 1917. Subsequently this was raised to seven years, although this goal was not fully realized in some rural and outlying districts. In 1958 Khrushchev instituted a program that added one year to both the seven- and 10-year schools, but the latter innovation was abandoned a few months before his dismissal in 1964.

IN the early years of the Soviet regime there was much experimenting with progressive methods of education. Formal examinations were few, classroom discipline was lax, and students were even encouraged to criticize their teachers. But Stalin, who had been a student in a Tbilisi seminary for five years, was unimpressed by these methods and ordered a return to conservative teaching practices. Today discipline in Soviet schools is strict. Teaching techniques emphasize memorization and long homework assignments even in the primary grades. The children are taught mathematics from the first grade on, and every student is required to select a second language for study in the fifth grade. Textbooks and curricula are the same throughout the country. American educators have often criticized the rigidity of the Soviet educational system, arguing that it stifles individual student initiative. On the other hand, at the end of the required eight years, the youngsters have learned a considerable amount.

All Russian children attend school six days a week; the graduate of a 10-year Soviet school has had more hours of classroom education than has an American high-school graduate. He has studied a foreign language for six years and has been introduced to physics, chemistry and astronomy. The student who has done well can take a competitive examination for entrance to a technical school or university. If he qualifies, his education will continue for another four to six years.

Out of the 3.5 million students who had finished their secondary education in 1964, some 820,000—about 23 per cent—were accepted by institutions of higher education. Of this number, more than 100,000 were enrolled in evening courses, and the rest were almost equally divided among full-time and correspondence courses. Space is at a premium in Soviet technical schools and universities; as a result many qualified students cannot be admitted to campus residence. The correspondence courses therefore play an important part in the Soviet educational system, drawing their students not only from the young, but also from older, unskilled workers who hope that additional training will enable them to move up the vocational ladder.

The next step in formal education, as in the United States, is graduate school, which offers a degree that falls between our master's and doctor's in status. According to most scholars, Soviet higher education compares favorably with higher education in the most advanced countries of the world.

THE chief vice of the Soviet educational system is its endless, pervasive emphasis on Marxism. On the primary-school level, the political indoctrination usually takes the form of slogans and textbook examples presenting an official moral, while systematic exposition of Communist theory and practice is a feature of secondary-school courses.

The majority of students in Soviet institutions of higher learning study the sciences rather than the humanities. Science majors are favored not only in the number of vacancies provided but also in the size of the stipends and in the rewards awaiting them. In addition, foreign students attending Soviet universities have reported that teaching standards in the sciences are far superior to those in law, economics and similar subjects that are not considered so important by the Kremlin leaders. The humanities suffer a further disadvantage

in that a dispassionate study of them involves repeated conflict with Communist political doctrines. But there is one humanities course that all university students must take each year. That is Marxism-Leninism, the study of Marxian doctrine. Every year students plow through the works of the two party prophets and attend lectures on the "science" of Marxism. Most of the students find the course a deadly bore.

IN odd contrast to the situation in the United States, where there has been widespread criticism of "life adjustment" courses, Russia's rigid, old-fashioned system of education recently came in for severe criticism by the Kremlin for its failure to prepare Soviet youngsters for adult life. The tremendous increase in the number of students seeking admission to universities, coupled with the country's labor shortage, prompted Khrushchev in 1958 to denounce Soviet youths' reluctance to "soil their hands in physical labor" and to endorse some proposals for making education more practical.

One proposal advanced by Khrushchev was that all students should go to work for a period of time after completing their schooling. This met with considerable resistance from educators, parents and leading scientists, and had not been put into effect by the time Khrushchev was dismissed. The recommendation had only one practical result: the student who works for a few years in his chosen field after graduation from secondary school is given preference in the evaluation of his entrance examination for admission to an institution of higher learning.

Most children between nine and 14 belong to the Pioneers, an organization something like the scouts in Western countries. Almost every community has its Pioneer Palace where the young are taught singing, dancing, camping and other activities. When they join the organization they take a solemn oath "to love the Soviet Union, to live, to study, and to fight according to the teachings of Lenin and . . . the Communist Party."

During the summer many Soviet youngsters go to Pioneer camps. Visitors to the Bratsk hydroelectric project several hundred miles north of Irkutsk in the Siberian wilderness may go by motorboat down the Angara River into the Siberian forest, where on a small backwater they will find a dock decorated with banners proclaiming the Bratsk Pioneer Camp.

On the dock a hundred Pioneers in shorts and white shirts, with triangular red kerchiefs neatly tied around their necks, are lined up. At a word from their commander they break into a stirring song of welcome. Later, they show their visitors the barracks and mess hall, the open-air theater and finally their fondest possession: two bear cubs that a local hunter caught in the forest nearby. These Pioneers are children of the workers at Bratsk.

Many Soviet youths between the ages of 15 and 26 belong to the Komsomol, or Communist Youth Organization. Here they are subjected to intense political indoctrination, and some undertake special assignments for the state, such as spreading party propaganda or opening up new lands for agriculture. The Komsomol is the testing ground for subsequent membership in the Communist Party.

THESE educational and political programs perform only a part of the task of bringing up younger people. In most parts of the world parents and usually the church play an equally important role. As noted in an earlier chapter, family life in the Soviet Union is severely restricted. But the Church's influence has suffered even more drastically.

Embracing the atheism of Marx, who had called religion the "opium of the people," the Communists have followed a militantly antireligious policy. One reason is that the Orthodox Church was an especially baneful influence in czarist Russia. Another was the Communists' conviction that their party could tolerate no rival for the loyalty of its followers. Because the Church's teachings were so diametrically opposed to the Communists' materialistic philosophy, it was potentially an even more dangerous rival than opposition political parties. From the beginning, therefore, the Soviet regime carried on a ruthless campaign of closing churches, arresting and exiling priests, and fostering a vigorous propaganda campaign against religious worship of all varieties. The campaign had a fair amount of success among young people, among urban intellectuals and among those who were forced by pressure to make peace with the regime. But the centuries-old hold of the Church was not entirely broken.

WHEN the Germans attacked Russia in 1941, Stalin saw that he must mobilize all forces to rally the country, and he sought to make peace with the Orthodox Church. He was aided by the readiness of the Church hierarchy to come to terms with the Communists. An accord was finally reached between the Kremlin and the acting Patriarch of Russia whereby the Church was allowed to publish religious books and a Church magazine and to reopen its theological schools. The antireligious propaganda campaign was relaxed. Other religious groups, including the Protestants, Moslems and Jews, were also granted respites.

The easing of antireligious oppression, coupled with the popular thirst for spiritual solace from the hardships of the war, fostered a limited religious revival in the Soviet Union. Churches were again crowded, while the priesthood for its part called upon the congregations to defend the country and support their atheistic ruler, Stalin, "with deep love and gratitude."

Since the war the Orthodox Church has continued to serve the Kremlin faithfully at home and abroad, and today it enjoys a measure of freedom to worship and safety from persecution. Other beliefs have fared less well. The Jews in particular have suffered periodic revivals of anti-Semitism, a phenomenon which in Russia had its antecedents under the czars.

The religious revival that began during the war continues. A visitor to the Baptist church in Moscow—the only Protestant house of worship in the capital—will find it packed with perhaps 2,000 people crowded into a building designed for a few hundred. Even the temporary balconies are a sea of devout faces. A closer look at any congregation in the Soviet Union, however, reveals that most of the worshipers are older people who were born and brought up before the Revolution, and nine out of 10 of them are women. In provincial cities one may find a slightly larger proportion of young people. But to interpret this as a sign of a mass religious revival would be misleading. As the older generation dies off, religion is likely to become even less of a force in Soviet life.

DESPITE the combined efforts of the party, the Pioneers and Komsomol, of the Soviet school system and the Soviet family, Russia today has a "youth problem" similar to that of Western nations. While the problem involves only a minority of Soviet youth, its symptoms are dramatically evident in this group.

The juvenile delinquents of New York and Chicago have their counterparts in Russia in the so-called "hooligans," whose name the Communists imported from the West. The hooligans are particularly troublesome in the major cities. These gangs, who infest the parks, movie houses and sports stadiums, are a product of boredom and of a lack of respect for the older generation that has been aggravated by the disruption of family life. Frequently the police have proved powerless to cope with them.

Typical of the incidents that have occurred was one in Leningrad, where an outstanding student from Moscow University remonstrated with a gang of hooligans who were brawling in a public park. The hoodlums drew knives and stabbed the student to death.

These boys were subsequently apprehended, tried and shot. But similar outrages continued until authorities proposed that the party organize posses of vigilantes, or auxiliary police, to patrol the public parks and streets in groups of five or six, especially during holidays. The response was immediate. Units were made up not only of party members but of nonparty citizens. So long as these so-called *Druzhinniki* stick to the job of apprehending hooligans, their activities are accepted and endorsed by their fellow citizens. But like members of other vigilante groups, they are often no more than officious busybodies. Then they are viewed much as their counterparts would be in the United States: with irritation and resentment.

In contrast to the hooligans, Russia's *stilyagi* (style hounds) are more or less peaceable citizens. Like their style-conscious counterparts in the United States and Great Britain, the *stilyagi* seem to be motivated chiefly by a desire to attract attention. Their method of self-expression is to wear odd clothes: tight pants, strange hats and gaudy neckties. They can be seen in any restaurant that has an orchestra, even in Moscow's staid, ultraconservative National Hotel.

The *stilyagi* are not a menace, but they are an indication of the ferment that has attacked Soviet youth. The great majority of young Russians are restless and dissatisfied with the world they are inheriting. They are indifferent to the Communist faith that their parents embraced, although they do have great pride in the Soviet Union as a nation.

FAR more important, many young people are seeking the less material benefits of a civilized Western community: wider knowledge of contemporary art, music and literature, and the right to think and write and talk as they please. At times they have even openly questioned the party's propaganda efforts. Their restlessness in the days of the Hungarian revolt in 1956 led to stirrings and demonstrations within Moscow University, with such effect that Khrushchev himself felt compelled to go to the great gleaming temple of learning on Lenin Hills and read the student body the riot act. Any further unauthorized demonstrations, said the First Secretary, would be severely punished.

The hooligans and the *stilyagi* may be temporary afflictions similar to those found in the younger generation of every modern country. But the discontent among the larger body of youth goes deep. Though it is hardly likely to erupt into open defiance, it does demonstrate how the Communist Party, with all its propaganda apparatus, has failed to create that long-promised hero—the New Soviet Man.

*Kissing the icon of St. Sergius, a woman venerates the patron saint of Russia at the monastery named for him near Moscow.*

# Target: Mind and Soul

The minds of Russia's citizens are a continuing target for Government persuasion. Party dogma is omnipresent. Although more criticism of officialdom is permitted in newspapers now than in the past, the press remains a Government organ. And although artists are freer to express themselves, the art that wins state backing reflects "correct" views. The Orthodox Church operates more freely than in the early days of Communism. But atheism remains the official state position; and even the Church, like the educational system, is used to inculcate patriotism.

THE CENTER OF FAITH *for devout Russians for six
centuries has been the Monastery of the Holy Trinity and St. Sergius,
in Zagorsk, where Church tradition decrees an elaborate ritual*

**AT COMMUNION** in the Zagorsk Monastery of the Holy
Trinity and St. Sergius (*opposite*), a priest partakes of
wine before cutting the bread and placing it in the chalice.

**PATRIARCH ALEXIS,** the spiritual head of Russia's Orthodox Church, wears a cross-topped miter while seated before the opened altar screen (*background*) at Zagorsk.

# WIDESPREAD EDUCATION *is one of the state's proud achievements*

**TOURING THE HERMITAGE,** Soviet schoolgirls (*above*) view one of the world's great art collections. It includes paintings by the masters and gold objects from Scythia.

**DURING FINAL EXAMS,** students from the local university crowd the library (*opposite*) at Baku on the Caspian Sea. The inevitable portrait of Lenin shows him reading *Pravda*.

RAISING ARMS, children in a Moscow primary school imitate clouds and lightning as the teacher describes the weather. School uniforms, which were standard up until the Revolution, have been brought back again by the state gradually in the years since 1936.

123

# MEDICAL STUDENT, *Nelya Spiridonova, one of more than 100,000 girls who study medicine each year, puts in a long day at Siberia's Irkutsk Medical College*

**A CHEST EXAMINATION** is carried out by Nelya. It takes about six years to obtain a medical degree in Russia. Training begins at about the time Americans start college.

**A TEST OF REFLEXES**, performed by Nelya, is carefully supervised by a woman member of the faculty. About 60 per cent of all of Russia's medical students are girls.

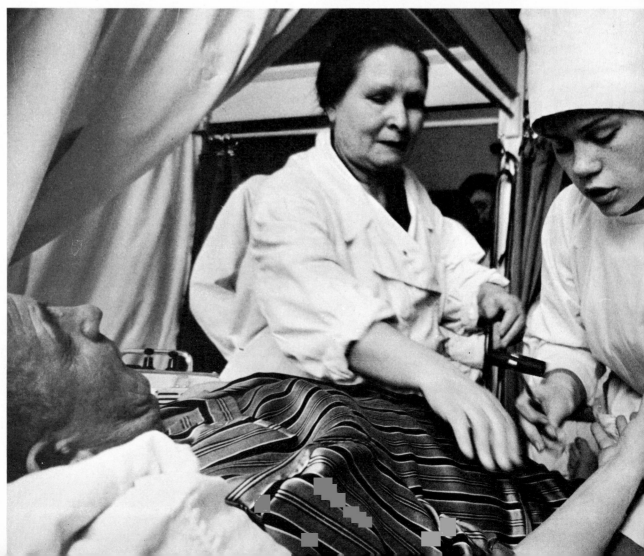

**IN HER DORMITORY** after classes with two of her three roommates, Nelya waters plants (*above*). Nelya spends an average of three hours a day in study hall and 30 hours a week in classes and laboratories.

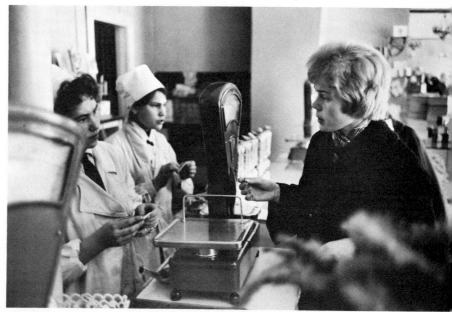

**AT A FOOD STORE,** Nelya buys a box of candy (*above*) for her roommates. During part of her free time, she manages to study ballet.

**AT LUNCH** Nelya joins two friends (*below*) in a cafeteria. Lunch is her big meal of the day; supper usually consists of cheese and bread.

**THE LIFE OF YOUTH** *is strongly influenced by the state. The Government provides daytime nursery schools for the very young and organizes a thoroughgoing physical fitness program*

**DANCING,** preschool children whose parents are employed in a gas plant near Moscow pass the day in a state-supported factory nursery.

**CAMPING** near Leningrad (*below*), Pioneers take part in a scouting exercise. Competitions were held in tent-pitching, hiking and cooking.

**BROWSING**, students gather at a Moscow University bookstall. Tolstoi, Chekhov and Gorki sell very well, but the only foreign authors available are those whose works are approved by the state.

PERFECTIONISM is the hall-mark of Bolshoi dancers like the one opposite. Fifteen hundred apply for entrance to the Bolshoi's school each year; 30 to 40 are accepted.

# The Thaw in Arts and Letters

AN old Russian legend tells of an impoverished noblewoman who wanted to refurbish her large, bare palace in St. Petersburg. Unable to afford the usual marble statuary, she had one of her handsomest serf girls frozen in ice and set up in the foyer of the palace.

Many observers maintain that during the rule of Joseph Stalin Russia's arts and literature, like the serf girl, were frozen in ice. Though they are still rigidly encased, in recent years there have been signs that the ice is beginning to melt.

A widespread impression in the West has been that Russian culture exists only on the surface of Russian life. This belief holds that artists and writers have been deprived of influence on the upper levels of power by the autocracy of both the czars and the Communists and that they have been prevented until recently by the nationwide illiteracy from reaching the Soviet people. The impression is false. Although

Russian writers have failed to instigate a successful liberal political movement, their influence has been profound in the formation of liberal thought and in the enunciation of the national identity and purpose.

Despite the illiteracy of the past, Russian authors have always enjoyed a large, avid and attentive audience, which the Kremlin's mass education drive has further enlarged. From the poetry of Pushkin to the novels of Dostoevski, Russian literature has been acclaimed throughout the world for generations. Nowhere today are books printed in such quantities as in the Soviet Union. New editions of the great Russian classics, from Gogol to Gorki, are snapped up overnight, and the works of such contemporary poets as Yevgeni Yevtushenko and Andrei Voznesensky are generally sold out months before publication. A 20-volume edition of Tolstoi's collected works, of which 17 have been published, sold out a printing of 700,000 copies by advance subscription. In the Moscow subway one often finds half the passengers immersed not in newspapers or popular magazines but in copies of the works of such authors as Turgenev, Chekhov or Pushkin. Book prices are modest. Hard-cover books seldom cost more than one dollar, and many cost only half that much.

THE enthusiasm for culture extends far beyond literature. The U.S.S.R. has 481 professional theaters, including 35 for opera and ballet. In addition, Moscow and other large cities are dotted with auditoriums, sometimes run-down and unheated, but frequently filled to overflowing by audiences eagerly listening to readings of poetry or the Russian classics.

The ballet is the supreme example of Russian achievement in the performing arts, and its cathedral, Moscow's Bolshoi Theater, seldom has an empty seat. The tradition is an old one, dating from the day in the 18th Century when Catherine the Great brought the Italian choreographer Angiolini to St. Petersburg to teach the imperial ballet. Ever since then the Bolshoi has been the pride of all Russians.

Each year hundreds of children apply for admission to the Bolshoi's ballet school, but only 30 to 40 are accepted. For nine years the lucky ones take regular educational courses and practice dancing assiduously at the same time. Then, in a final test before the directors of the Bolshoi and other ballet companies of the country, their future is decided. The Bolshoi gets its choice of the best. Those it rejects are snapped up by the ballets in provincial capitals.

ASIDE from literature and the performing arts, Russia has given the world some of its greatest musicians. Its contemporary composers include the late Sergei Prokofiev, who began his career before the Revolution, Dmitri Shostakovich and Aram Khachaturyan. They and others continued to write during Stalin's repressive era, although their works were frequently banned by his censors. Today a number of young composers are experimenting with new forms of music, as are their contemporaries in the West.

The harnessing of all Russian culture to the Communist machine dates back almost to the Revolution. Lenin had said: "Socialist proletariat literature cannot be an instrument of gain for persons or groups; it cannot altogether be an individual matter, independent of the whole proletarian cause. Down with nonparty writers!" In the 1920s, however, literary works were not severely censored; only anti-Communist writings were forbidden and a number of inventive writers made their appearance. The literary giant of the period was Vladimir Mayakovski, who committed suicide in 1930. In addition to his fine lyrical poetry, Mayakovski turned out propagandistic doggerel for the party. But he also wrote stinging satires of the Soviet bureaucracy.

In the 1930s Stalin began to cut down on the free expression of ideas. When the Union of Writers was founded in 1932, Stalin's henchmen used it to control the literary intelligentsia. All prominent writers had to join the union.

The crackdown was at first relatively mild. When Mikhail Bulgakov, a non-Communist writer and author of one of the few great post-revolutionary plays, *The Days of the Turbins,* found his works being banned and his plays removed from the stage, he asked Stalin for permission to leave the country. As a writer, he said, he had no place on the Soviet scene. Stalin denied his request. The regime, said Stalin, needed all the talents it had. Like a benign father he advised Bulgakov to adapt himself to the Soviet rules. Then he raised the ban on some of Bulgakov's works, appointed him assistant director of the Moscow Art Theater —perhaps the greatest theater in the world— and sent the playwright on his way unharmed.

But Stalin's good humor did not last long. As the terror grew, many writers went into obscurity or were shot, until only the works of hacks and scribblers were published.

AS his power became absolute, Stalin extended his control over the entire cultural life of the nation, imposing his tastes on writers and composers. When Shostakovich's works displeased him he sent the young man off to Archangel in the far north for a few months, scolding him for his "formalism."

Stalin's precept for creative art was "socialist realism." Although still officially in force today, the precept never has been clearly defined. But generally it means that only those themes that contribute to strengthening socialism should be dealt with. Novels should describe how a Soviet factory exceeds its production quota, how a collective farm increases its yield or how a border guard's vigilance thwarts capitalist saboteurs. The heroes of socialist realism should be "positive," i.e., noble prototypes of the New Soviet Man. Villains should be "negative," i.e., wholly bad. To demonstrate the superiority of the Soviet system, the hero should always win and the villain lose. Complex love stories or themes involving the inner conflicts of individuals are frowned upon.

"Realism" applies to the way a story is told, a piece of music is composed or a picture is painted. Music should be tuneful. Painting should be purely representational. All creative works should depict "socialist truth"—life as the Kremlin would like it to be.

Except for a brief wartime relaxation, Stalin's insistence on "socialist realism" dominated Russian writing for 20 years. A few authors stopped writing for publication altogether. Boris Pasternak, Russia's greatest 20th Century poet, withdrew from public life and devoted himself to poetry and fiction that he knew could not be published and earned his living by translating Shakespeare and other foreign classics into Russian. Other writers dutifully turned out the monotonous drivel to which Soviet literature had descended.

By 1953, when Stalin died, it was only reasonable to assume that 30 years of repression and censorship had completely crushed the creative arts. But this was far from true. Voices soon began to be heard, timid at first but then louder and more eloquent. Taking advantage of the dilemma facing the party censors—pledged to eliminate Stalinist repression but determined not to relinquish control over the arts—the intellectuals pressed forward with their demands for greater freedom of expression. The course of their campaign has not been smooth. But they have refused to give up the struggle.

THE first voice was that of Ilya Ehrenburg, a former émigré who had returned from Paris to Russia in the '30s. His short novel *The Thaw* was published in 1954. In it Ehrenburg dared to discuss such dangerous topics as Stalin's terror and the purges. He even attacked official Soviet art as "philistine."

In 1956 an unknown young writer, Vladimir Dudintsev, published an even sharper attack. Although his novel, *Not by Bread Alone,* was of modest artistic merit, its political daring brought it enthusiastic attention throughout Russia. Soon a number of Soviet journals began publishing poetry and prose equally critical and of much higher literary quality.

Party officials in the Writers' Union grumbled but took no active steps to quiet the unorthodox voices. But the 1956 uprisings in Poland and Hungary made them change their approach. These rebellions, which had been instigated largely by intellectuals, gave rise to fears of similar unrest at home. The writers were called on to stop their criticisms and to comply with the Stalinist ritual of confession. Some submitted, but the more stalwart refused.

Infuriated by this defiance, Khrushchev summoned the holdouts to his *dacha* near Moscow and told them he would use force if they did not give in. "My hand will not tremble," he said ominously.

Shortly thereafter, most of the writers reluctantly made their ritual confessions, and Dudintsev "revised" his novel. A few remained adamant and stopped writing for publication.

THE next crisis occurred in 1957, with the publication of Boris Pasternak's now famous *Dr. Zhivago,* a complex novel dealing with a Russian intellectual's unenthusiastic reaction to the Revolution. Because Soviet publishers were hesitant about accepting it, Pasternak submitted it to a publishing house in Italy. After its publication there, it appeared throughout the world, translated into many languages. To make matters worse, Pasternak was awarded the Nobel Prize in 1958 for his lifework. He accepted it. But six days later he turned it down. "In view of the meaning given to this honor in the community to which I belong," he wrote, he felt that he must convey his "voluntary refusal." Although Pasternak was expelled from the Writers' Union, many of his colleagues refused to join the attack. Throughout the world, Communist and non-Communist intellectuals were horrified by this turn of events. Their reaction startled the Kremlin and the attack subsided.

Reluctant to make martyrs of the other "liberal" writers or to antagonize their friends abroad, the Kremlin eased its control. Almost at once a new wave of bold, nonconformist literature began to enliven Soviet journals. Russian readers were delighted by the original and often complex verse of Yevtushenko and Voznesensky, and by the work of Victor Nekrasov, an older writer whose essays on foreign travel included blunt demands for greater literary freedom and sharp criticism of Soviet publishers for their failure to publish the works of such famous Westerners as Proust, Kafka and Joyce.

Published in editions of hundreds of thousands, works like these were eagerly received by the reading public. Their popularity forced the party leaders to give ground. Reluctantly, they permitted the publication of liberal magazines and of the works of a few previously banned foreign writers. They even rehabilitated Communist writers whom Stalin had denounced.

But the freedom did not last. Late in 1962 Khrushchev decided that the situation had got out of hand. He and Leonid Ilyichev, head of the Central Committee's Ideological Commission, demanded that the party expel several popular writers, including Nekrasov, the leader of the resistance. Yevtushenko was forbidden to travel abroad, and others were sent to "production sites" in Siberia. Liberal editors were fired and obedient old hacks given their jobs.

Again there were token recantations. Again the reaction abroad was bitterly hostile. And again the attack subsided. It had accomplished little. Few writers were expelled from the party, and those who had been sent to the provinces were permitted to return home, where they continued ignoring the rules and finding outlets for their works in such journals as *Novi mir* and *Yunost,* a magazine for youth.

At the same time, the orthodox Stalinist writers and editors continued to hold their positions. They were especially strong in the provinces, where they established their own journals. The Government, anxious to have as many mouthpieces as possible, encouraged them with large allotments of paper. But their publications were unpopular and unprofitable.

BY the time Khrushchev was ousted an uneasy truce prevailed between the two camps. The Stalinists continued to write for a dwindling public. The liberals continued to publish their magazines. Today, the truce is still on, and one further hopeful step has been taken. In 1965 Ilyichev was dismissed from his post, and some of his functions were turned over to one of the ablest and most influential members of the Presidium, P. N. Demichev.

In other branches of art a similar though not so pronounced development has taken place. The great majority of dramas still cling to the old conventions, but a few more daring plays have appeared recently. In the spring of 1965 Moscow audiences laughed uproariously at a series of satiric sketches presented by a Yiddish vaudeville troupe. In June of that year *Pravda,* the official party newspaper, reversed its previous condemnation of a recent play about the Kronshtadt mutiny, the naval revolt in 1921 against the Soviet Government. In painting, a handful of men have experimented with Abstract art. In music, young composers are writing material that cannot be performed under present rules but that seems to assuage their thirst for something new.

THE ballet of the Bolshoi Theater, the classical stronghold of Russian art, has also become more daring. Recently Stravinsky's *The Rite of Spring,* barred for more than half a century, was performed to a standing ovation.

What has been the impact of these developments on the Soviet public and what is their implication for the future?

Among the middle classes the effect has probably been slight. Most factory managers have little time to worry about the problems of the creative artist. Nor are they aware of the low level to which cultural standards have fallen. But in Soviet cultural life there is another audience, younger in tastes though not necessarily in years. This audience includes elderly professors whose esthetic standards and tastes were already established when the Revolution broke out. But it also includes young students to whom current Soviet literature seems crass and stultified in comparison to the 19th Century classics and the Western books that they have managed to read. They know they cannot return to a bygone tradition. But why, they ask, can they not move forward in search of new forms, new ideas and new methods?

Like almost all Soviet citizens, these questioning youths are proud of their country and its scientific and economic progress. But as their material needs cease to preoccupy them, they search for greater latitude of self-expression in the world of ideas.

ONE episode, though not typical, shows the changes produced by the thaw. Valeri Tarsis was a minor writer who survived Stalin by publishing only innocuous translations and commentaries. However, he was convinced of the incompatibility of the Communist system with freedom of thought. After Stalin's death he tried to publish his views in Soviet journals. His manuscripts were repeatedly rejected. Finally he smuggled abroad a number of open attacks on the Communist system and the party that were published in England.

The Soviet leaders, reluctant to break their pledge not to imprison recalcitrant writers, had him declared insane and sent to an asylum. When Tarsis' friends abroad discovered his fate they protested to Khrushchev. They were even joined by a few Soviet writers. Khrushchev retreated and Tarsis was released. Thereupon the invincible old writer sat down and wrote a novel—*Ward 7*—about his experiences in the asylum. In it he denounced Khrushchev by name and urged all honest Russians to rid themselves of Communism. Never since the Revolution had such a violent attack been launched. Yet in 1965, when Tarsis' second book had been published in both Britain and the U.S., the Kremlin did nothing. And this in the face of Tarsis' insistence that his name and his address and telephone number appear in the book.

Tarsis is not typical of "liberal" Soviet writers, nor do others share his dream of ousting the Communists. But he has become a symbol of the right of every Soviet citizen to say what he believes—and survive.

The serf girl is still frozen in her case of ice, but in the warmer atmosphere of the post-Stalin era the ice is melting slowly. If ever it cracks, it may well pose some perplexing problems for the men in the Kremlin.

RENOWNED WRITER, Boris Pasternak gardens at his home near Moscow (*above*) during the debate over his novel, *Doctor Zhivago*. He died in 1960.

POPULAR POET, Yevgeni Yevtushenko recites his works in Moscow's Mayakovski Square (*above*). His poems of protest made him a hero of youth.

GREAT VIOLINIST, David Oistrakh gives a lesson in Moscow's Conservatory (*below, left*). He has won acclaim in the West as well as in the Soviet Union.

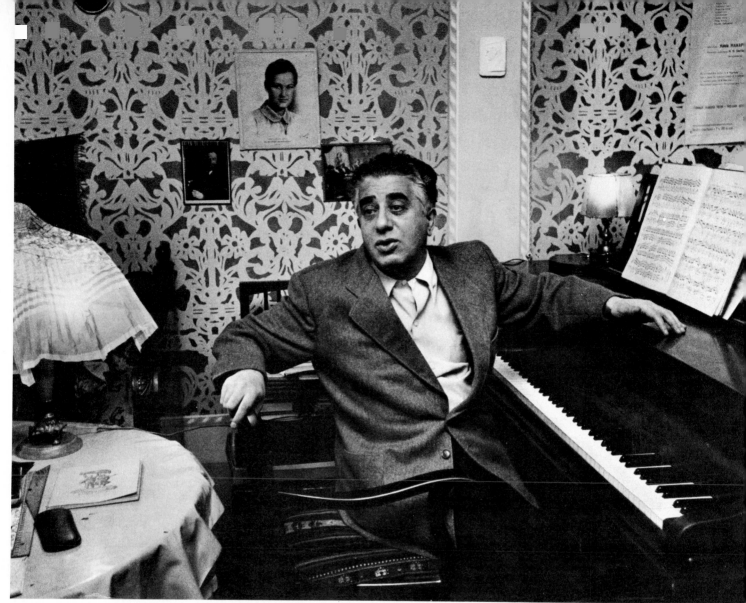

*Once attacked for composing "bourgeois music," Aram Khachaturyan has since made a fortune from ballet scores and other works.*

# Proud Heritage of a Rich and Living Culture

Russian culture—from the Middle Ages until most recent times—has been one of impressive richness. A splendid religious art flourished in Kiev before the Tatar invasion. Arts and letters received new impetus with Peter the Great's "Westernization" drive in the early part of the 18th Century. In the following century a literary renaissance began with the classical poetry of Pushkin. Later came the masterful novels of Dostoevski, Turgenev and Tolstoi; the evocative plays of Chekhov; and the romantic music of Tchaikovsky and Rachmaninov. Today, despite restraints, this tradition is carried on by world-renowned artists like those shown here.

135

MASTERLY MOSAIC of an angel in the Cathedral of St. Sofia in Kiev is one of several that were probably done by Greek artists.

CHURCH ART *shone above all other forms in old Russia because of the rich tradition which came to southern Russia from Byzantium almost a thousand years ago. The characteristic onion-shaped domes of Orthodox churches were developed by native architects in northern Russia*

GILDED DOMES of Our Saviour's Cathedral in Moscow are topped by elaborately embellished crosses. The drums supporting the domes are decorated with colored tiles.

LAVISH INTERIOR of Kiev's Cathedral of St. Vladimir (*opposite*) is rich in paintings. Built in the 19th Century, St. Vladimir's was modeled after early Kievan churches.

A CLASH IN PAINTING *persists in the Soviet Union. The state prefers "socialist realism"—poster art for political propaganda. But young Russian painters want to express personal feelings and are trying Abstractionism*

**OFFICIAL ART** is typified by a canvas showing Lenin speaking during Bolshevik power seizure in 1917. The painting, by V. A. Serov, is prominently displayed in a Moscow museum, where crowds throng past it.

**PERSONAL ART** in an extreme idiom is exemplified by the frenzied self-portrait of a young painter, Anatoly Zverev. The picture is kept in Zverev's closet. He has never exhibited in Russia and sells only to friends.

139

**PERFORMING ARTS** *are regimented on a huge scale by the Soviet Ministry of Culture, which uses them for indoctrination while appeasing the people's ravenous hunger for culture*

A POLITICAL "WESTERN" is filmed by a state movie company. The film deals with "the coming of Soviet power to Kirgizia." The Bolsheviks are the good guys and their opponents are outlaws.

A "DECADENT" OPERETTA, *Sylva* by Imre Kallman, is put on in Moscow. Such light Viennese entertainment is extremely popular, and Soviet officialdom tolerates it.

TOP CULTURAL SHOWPLACE, Moscow's Bolshoi Theater (*opposite*) is jammed by bureaucrats, officers and foreigners for an opera. Most Bolshoi performances sell out.

**BALLET'S BEAUTY** is at a peak during a Bolshoi performance of *Swan Lake*. One of the most noted ballet companies in the world, the Bolshoi troupe works hard to maintain a classical tradition of impeccable technique and dazzling spectacle typical of an early 20th Century style.

143

CALISTHENICS at 7 a.m., to the commands from a loudspeaker, start the day at the Sanatorium of Miners in Sochi, a popular Black Sea resort built by the state.

# 9

# Collective Joy for the Multitudes

IN 1928, when the First Five-Year Plan was getting under way, the little town of Sochi on the Black Sea coastline consisted of a few run-down villas that had once belonged to the aristocracy, two or three third-rate hotels, a public restaurant and a public bathhouse. But on a hillside overlooking the sea the white walls of a big new sanatorium for the Red Army were rising among the pines. The sanatorium was a portent of Sochi's future development as the most important resort town of the U.S.S.R.

Overlooking the sea on each side of the town are nearly 80 palaces of rest set in statue-studded parks. Most of them affect the wedding-cake architecture of Stalin's day, but the newer ones exhibit the austere lines that were developed under Khrushchev. Although Sochi is the most popular of Russia's Black Sea resorts, it is only one of several. The coast, from Batum in the north to Odessa in the south, is dotted with sanatoriums and rest homes.

The Black Sea coast is a verdant, lush and extraordinarily beautiful area. Before the Revolution it was Russia's Riviera, the playground of the country's aristocracy. One of the sanatoriums was originally the palace of Czar Nicholas II. This building is in Yalta, a city that later gained fame as the site of a World War II summit conference in 1945 attended by Roosevelt, Churchill and Stalin. Not far from the Czar's former home is the palace of Prince Mikhail Vorontsov, the 19th Century Governor of the region who first brought the Black Sea coast into fashion. Several other ornate palaces and villas still stand, cheek by jowl with the mass-produced Soviet structures.

---

**WORLD CHESS CHAMPIONS**

| | | |
|---|---|---|
| 1921-27 | Jose R. Capablanca | Cuba |
| 1927-35 | Alexander A. Alekhine | France |
| 1935-37 | Max Euwe | Netherlands |
| 1937-46 | Alexander A. Alekhine | France |
| 1946-48 | (Vacant) | |
| 1948-57 | Mikhail Botvinnik | U.S.S.R. |
| 1957-58 | Vassily Smyslov | U.S.S.R. |
| 1958-60 | Mikhail Botvinnik | U.S.S.R. |
| 1960-61 | Mikhail Tal | U.S.S.R. |
| 1961-63 | Mikhail Botvinnik | U.S.S.R. |
| 1963- | Tigran Petrosian | U.S.S.R. |

RUSSIAN PREDOMINANCE in chess is shown on the list above. Alexander Alekhine, world champion for 17 years, was an expatriate Russian who played for France.

---

Along the Sochi sea front an asphalt promenade is crowded with strollers. Like crowds in any health resort they appear bored to death. Occasionally they glance in the windows of souvenir shops. One shop advertises "spoken letters." Here vacationers can make recordings that extend greetings to their families at home. Another sells colored glass vases. Several display bottles of Soviet brandy and champagne.

A little knot of vacationers is huddled about a bench in the park by the sea, watching a chess game with fascinated interest as the players hunch over the board deep in concentration,

oblivious of the kibitzers around them. Chess is classified as a sport in the Soviet Union and is one of Russia's favorite pastimes. At the annual international championship, which is generally held in Moscow, Russians are almost invariably the winners.

TO the average Soviet factory worker the prices of the souvenirs on sale at Sochi would seem staggering, but Sochi's window-shoppers are not average. Most of them belong to the privileged middle class, although they also include some skilled workers from the factories in the north who have been rewarded for exceeding their production quotas by being given a vacation by the seaside.

Still others are vacationers from far-off Siberia: engineers, geologists and technicians who are generally kept in their remote jobs for two years and then given a six-month vacation. In the distant north country there are few ways of spending the extra money they have earned for working in the wilderness. Now their pockets are bulging with rolls of cash they have saved for the great splurge. Like the prospectors of America's Far West a century ago who would burst into San Francisco after a year or two in the mountains, they are making up for the long months of boredom with a well-earned spree.

In the evenings they congregate in the numerous restaurants along the coast, where jazz bands blare out as modern a rhythm as the Soviet authorities permit.

In Russia the word "sanatorium" is applied to many institutions in addition to hospitals and convalescent homes. It also refers to rest and recreation homes. Most of the visitors to Sochi do not stay at the sanatoriums but at one of several new hotels that are operated by the state. Others stay in boardinghouses run by the townspeople.

The occupants of the sanatoriums are principally there to convalesce from heart, nerve or kidney troubles or some other ailment. Others are there simply to rest. All follow rigid daily routines: early breakfasts, gentle walks, long rests and bus rides to the sulphur baths near the shore, where they are given their treatments. They have an early supper and hear the call of "lights out" just when the Sochi restaurants are waking up for the night.

The standard cure at the sanatoriums lasts precisely 28 days, and the price ranges from 120 to 180 rubles. Although this represents a great deal of money to the average Soviet worker, he seldom has to pay the total himself. Tickets for the stay are usually given out by the trade unions, which may contribute up to 70 per cent of the cost.

Along the coast south of Sochi the road leads between high, green-painted fences. Occasionally through an open gate one catches a glimpse of a luxurious villa set among well-kept lawns and overlooking the sea. Here Russia's highest officials and richest citizens pass their summer vacations in sumptuous comfort and in strict isolation from the lower classes.

About four million Soviet citizens spend their vacations on the sunny beaches of the Black Sea coast. Nearly one million go to Sochi, which can accommodate 44,000 people at a time.

IT is unlikely that as much as 2 per cent of the Soviet population enjoys the privilege of vacationing in one of the Black Sea resorts. The ordinary peasant, of course, takes what leisure he can get during the long winter months when the fields are deep in snow and the cattle snug in the barn back of the hut. This is the time for rest on the collective farms, and for carving the gingerbread panels that decorate the little rural houses.

The great majority of urban workers spend their month's vacation at home or at odd jobs that they take to supplement their meager incomes. Some of them rent a room in a country *dacha*. But the young people—the most favored group in all Russian society—are well provided with amusements on the athletic fields and in the stadiums that are the boast of every modern Russian city.

Even Stalin, who starved and harried his subjects, recognized the importance to the country of a sound, healthy youth. As early as the 1930s the urban youth were encouraged to join athletic clubs at school or in the universities, in the Pioneers or the Komsomol, or in the factories. Today sports facilities in Soviet cities are fully as good as those in U.S. cities.

EACH city has many clubs where volleyball, soccer, track and gymnastics are organized and taught. In the long winters skating and cross-country skiing are favorite pastimes.

Potential athletes are quickly spotted by local coaches and trainers. If their talents warrant, they are usually transferred to special physical-culture institutes or to schools that specialize in athletic training. Though they are expected to continue their academic studies in these institutions, or to coach younger athletes if they have already completed their own education, they are given special facilities and all the time they need for training. If they reach the championship category they are placed under the best trainers and coaches the country can provide. This emphasis on sports has paid off. The Russians are excellent athletes. In the 1964 Olympics the U.S.S.R. took 35 bronze and 31 silver medals, and the 30 gold medals the Russians captured made the U.S.S.R. second only to the United States.

In prerevolutionary Russia sports were the exclusive prerogative of the aristocracy and wealthy groups and consisted chiefly of hunting and horse racing. Except for such traditional children's games as *lapta*, which resembles baseball, the majority of people had no opportunity whatever to participate in sports. And so when athletic competitions on a mass basis were introduced after the Revolution, the participants were understandably unfamiliar with the concepts of good sportsmanship and fair play.

Today, however, the ethics of sportsmanship are drilled into young athletes. In the Olympics and other international competitions Soviet athletes have generally shown that they can be good losers as well as good winners.

For many years before the Revolution, Russia and the United States had a long and close relationship on the trotting track. Until the construction of railroads both countries were handicapped by long distances and bad roads. In many areas the roads were so poor that heavy stagecoaches could not be used for transportation. Both countries therefore developed fast trotting horses capable of pulling light carriages for long distances. With the Revolution, however, private ownership of race horses was abolished in the Soviet Union, and for many years thereafter American horses were not raced in Russia. But in the summer of 1964 an international trotting race was held at the Hippodrome, Moscow's race track. The winner in a field of eight was an American horse, Apex Hanover. The Russians now own the six-year-old trotter, having acquired it in exchange for seven state-owned Orlov trotters. These Russian trotters, though not as fast as their American counterparts, are somewhat stronger and heavier. They were developed in Russia during the reign of Catherine the Great and were named for Count Grigori Orlov, one of her personal favorites and an advocate of improvement in the living conditions of the serfs. In recent years Russian horses, both thoroughbreds and trotters, have competed in international races in the United States, at both Yonkers and Roosevelt Raceways.

THE most popular spectator sport in the Soviet Union today is soccer, which occupies a position similar to that of baseball in the United States. Almost every provincial city has a team in either the "A" (major) or the "B" (minor) League, and in the larger towns there are often several clubs organized within factories, unions or even Government ministries. Thus the Torpedo Club belongs to the ZIL auto factory and "Dynamo" is the club of the internal security forces. Each club has teams participating in a number of sports, but the most important is invariably the soccer team.

Although the Soviet authorities describe all athletes as amateurs, good soccer players enjoy many of the prerogatives that professional ballplayers do in America. They are not bought and sold by their clubs, but they receive special privileges and high salaries and the organizations that ostensibly employ them seldom ask them actually to report to work.

The Russian soccer fan is also as ubiquitous as the traditional American sports enthusiast— and just as demanding. In cities that have only one athletic club the team is often organized by the municipal authorities. This puts the chief local official in somewhat the same position as that of a U.S. college president. "If our team doesn't do well," the mayor of Tashkent once told a foreigner, "I'm in trouble."

A champion soccer player is as much a hero among Soviet youth as a big-league star is in the United States. In a Pioneer camp in the heart of Siberia a foreign visitor asked a small camper what he intended to be when he grew up. "An engineer," he said, "and a soccer player like Yashin." Lev Yashin is the Soviet Union's leading goalkeeper.

EVERY Soviet city has its theaters and movie houses, and every factory has a "Workers' Club," usually a drab reading room whose walls are covered with slogans urging greater output. Night clubs, however, have no place on the Soviet scene except insofar as their function is performed by a few restaurants where the richer members of the community try to dispel the drabness of everyday life. Moscow has a dozen plush restaurants, each representing a region of Russia and offering the specialties of that area. The Aragvi, for example, serves shashlik and Georgian wines. In the summertime a favorite place to dance is the roof of the Moskva Hotel, overlooking the Kremlin.

New Year's Eve is the great occasion for such establishments, and many of the capital's citizens reserve seats (not tables) at their favorite restaurant weeks in advance. The Metropole Hotel is a popular year-end gathering place for those who can afford to celebrate outside their homes. In a dining room reminiscent of an old glass-roofed railroad station, a large dance band plays from a high stage while the guests dance around a fountain in the center of the room.

Tables are set with elaborate prerevolutionary crystal brimming with Soviet champagne and ancient silver bowls filled with black caviar from Astrakhan. The really fashionable places, however, are the clubs—the House of Journalists, the House of Movie-Makers, the House of Writers.

But such luxury is for only a tiny fraction of the population. The great majority can afford at best a modest banquet in their crowded rooms.

The chief characteristic of Soviet Government-sponsored leisure is collectivity. The child in the Pioneer Palace is taught to prefer group dancing to individual ballroom dancing. The young sportsman gets his exercise as part of a team in a club. Unless he belongs to the privileged middle class the Black Sea vacationer is likely to be a mere digit in the sanatorium collective, riding to and from his mud baths in a bus. Even the hunter or the fisherman can get a license to shoot or angle only as a member of a group organized where he works. If he wants to go off on a hunting trip, his club assigns him and his fellows a camping area to which they are taken in the club's bus or truck.

The underlying reason for this collectivity is the Kremlin's aim to develop a society in which the group or community is the basic unit. Individuals and individuality are considered enemies of the ideal collective Communist society, and no effort is spared to press people into a conforming group in which personal tastes, like private property, are submerged and eventually, the state hopes, eradicated.

The average Russian has learned to accept this, and whether he wants to sing or climb mountains, plant trees or simply play chess he realizes he must join a party-sponsored club.

A STRONG feeling of individuality is, however, a marked characteristic of the ordinary Russian, who by tradition prefers the privacy of his family to any large social group. Despite the facilities that the Government has provided for organized sport, one of the most popular Sunday pastimes for a family is taking the trolley line to the edge of town and walking through the birch and pine forests. They have a picnic, and when the sun starts to go down they go home, the parents exhausted and sunburned, the children swollen by bee stings and weeping, but in the food hamper a large assortment of those most beloved of all Russian treasures, mushrooms.

Even high officials seem to prefer the small private pleasures to the organized fun of the community. The chief planner of the Ukraine, a senior Communist, had lunch one Saturday with a foreigner in Kiev but excused himself early, explaining that he had to hurry out to the suburbs to tend his little garden plot.

PERHAPS the most coveted possession a Soviet citizen can have is a private car in which to make excursions into the countryside. But thus far the Government has made no effort to satisfy this craving. For several years there was vague talk of plans for the mass production of cars. But nothing has come of it, and it is unlikely that the manufacture of small family cars will be significantly expanded in the near future. The standard Soviet passenger car, the Volga, which is about the size of an American compact car, sells for 5,600 rubles—more than $6,000 at the official rate of exchange. A smaller car, the Moskvich, is available for about $4,500. But neither is in much demand. The prices are far too high for the average citizen. When Khrushchev visited the United States in 1959, he commented on a San Francisco expressway traffic jam as "a terrific waste," particularly because most of the cars had only one person in them. There seems little chance that Russians will be driving one to a car very soon, or that they will drive their own cars when they go on vacations.

A young and ardent Communist interpreter who had accompanied a foreigner through the hygienic delights of a Sochi sanatorium was asked once whether he would not enjoy a cure there during his holiday.

"Not me!" he answered. "When I get a vacation I go off to a village with my wife just to be alone for a while."

# Varied Uses of Physical Activity

*Holiday boat-riders take a quick voyage around Lake*

**GYMNASTIC PAGEANTRY** opens a mammoth sport and fitness show called *Sportakiad* at Moscow's Lenin Stadium (*above*). Gymnasts carried models of Russian rockets.

**SUN-DRENCHED FIELD** outside Leningrad (*below*) brings out both leisurely weekend sunbathers and more active types who play a vigorous game of netless volleyball.

Participation in sports amounts to more than simple fun in the Soviet Union. Russian successes in recent Olympic competitions reflect the intense effort the nation puts into developing physical prowess—both to strengthen the U.S.S.R. and to demonstrate its strength to the world. Soviet athletes are becoming expert even at such traditionally non-Russian events as tennis and basketball. In 1959 the Government established the Union of Sports Societies and Organizations of the U.S.S.R. to interest more citizens in athletics; in the years since, the trade unions and Komsomol, which directs the program, have drawn millions of men and women into organized sports for the first time. Each morning in Russia setting-up exercises are conducted in factories, farms, villages and Government offices. Yet to many Russians the outdoor life is not a matter of state discipline and national glory but simply a form of enjoyment.

*Issyk-Kul in the Tien Shan mountains. Thousands of Russians vacation at the many health resorts that line the banks of the snow-fed lake.*

INDIVIDUAL ACTIVITY *is still preferred to the organized fun of the community. Boating, skating and strolling in the parks help fill the hours*

**DRIFTING,** two cheerful rowboaters take their ease at a resort. Rowboats are one of the most popular attractions at the Gorki Park of Culture and Rest in Moscow.

**GLIDING ALONG,** children take skating lessons (*opposite*) in a Leningrad park near an old church. Russia's skating season begins in early November and ends in April.

**HISTORICAL SIGHTSEEING** attracts a party of Russians to the two-room house (*above*) in the Georgian town of Gori where Joseph Stalin lived as a boy. Russians tour in great numbers.

**LAZY FISHING** preoccupies two solitary anglers perched above the Dnieper River. Fishing societies determine who may fish where and when.

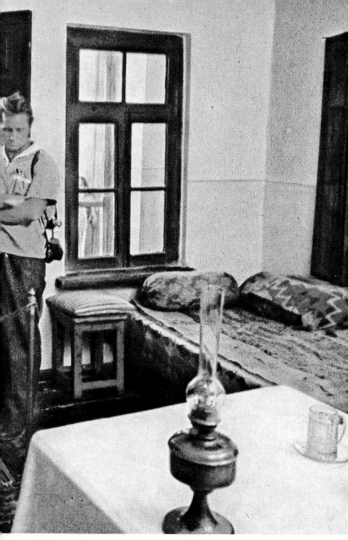

**CHESS AT TWILIGHT** absorbs casually garbed players (*below*) in the Park of Culture and Rest in Alma-Ata. The game is a national passion and the Russians produce world-champion masters.

**SWIMMING-HOLE FUN** delights a schoolboy playing above a canal constructed for boating and bathing in Leningrad's Kamenny Ostrov Park.

# PASSION FOR SPORTS *brings pleasure at home and honor abroad*

**SKILLED PLAYERS** stage a fast basketball game in a corner of Kiev's Dynamo Stadium (*above*). Basketball has been enjoying a boom throughout Russia since World War II. Some touring teams have beaten good U.S. opponents.

**SOARING GYMNAST,** Larisa Latynina, winner of nine gold medals in Olympic competitions, leaps high on a hill outside Moscow (*opposite*). Soviet women have dominated gymnastics since their debut at the 1952 Olympics.

**YOUTHFUL ROWERS,** well-trained Moscow girls, prepare to go out in their eight-oared shell (*right*). Soviet women athletes have regularly defeated European and American women in a variety of international athletic encounters.

GREAT SPORTS STADIUM looms white and spectral by Moscow's river (*above*). Named for Lenin, it houses athletic events throughout the year, in all kinds of weather.

SUNDAY SKIERS, the vanguard of the thousands who will turn out before the day is over, dot Moscow's Izmailovsky Park (*below left*), one of many ski centers. Since

the Russo-Finnish War of 1940, in which the Finnish ski troops held off nonskiing Russians, the sport has won hundreds of thousands of fans wherever there is snow.

TOBOGGAN SLIDE in a "Russian Hills" park offers roller-coaster rides and attracts skiers and strollers as well as sledders. Lights permit the slide to be used at night.

A WORKER handles a production-line job at the Gorki Automatic Tool Plant in Kiev, a factory completed in 1937 as a part of the Soviet industrialization drive.

# 10

# A Belligerent Neighbor

KARL MARX was still a student in 1835 when a brilliant French historian, Alexis de Tocqueville, called the attention of the world to the rise of two great new nations. One of these was dedicated to freedom; the other was founded on servitude. "The conquests of the American are . . . gained by the plowshare," he wrote, "those of the Russian by the sword."

The Soviet Union is openly and formally dedicated to the victory of Communism all over the world. Will it eventually win, as its leaders constantly predict? Or will it perhaps gradually lose its militancy and become content to live side by side with other systems? Or will it change its doctrines and adopt a less extreme form of government?

Lenin, the strategist of Russian Marxism, believed that Communism could triumph if the workers of the world rose against their capitalist governments and that state after state, beginning with Germany, would establish a Communist system. But, he warned, before the last great capitalist states succumbed they would resort to war against Communism. Stalin, less sanguine about the rising of the workers, determined to build a strong state that could defend itself under any circumstances.

FACED with the chance of nuclear war, Khrushchev abandoned the thesis that war was inevitable. "One cannot repeat," he once stated, "what the great Lenin said in completely different historical conditions without considering the concrete situation and the change in the balance of forces on a world scale."

By repudiating a fundamental tenet of Lenin's doctrine Khrushchev may well have weakened Marxism by opening to question its claim to eternal verity and infallibility. Yet he did not renounce the ultimate goal of world revolution.

Indeed, as his Cuban adventure demonstrated, he was still ready to go to the brink of war in order to place his chief adversary, the United States, under his nuclear guns. Khrushchev's humiliating defeat at that time may well have taught his successors a lesson—that nuclear war is not worth gambling with.

Yet despite Khrushchev's declaration that the Communist world could pursue a policy of "peaceful coexistence" with its adversaries, and eventually win the struggle by demonstrating to the world, and particularly to the new nations, that Communism was superior to capitalism, neither he nor his successors discarded their arsenal of revolutionary weapons. Though condemning nuclear war as suicide, the Soviet leaders have declared that "wars of liberation" are justified, and in Vietnam they have demonstrated how effectively subversion, terror and guerrilla warfare can paralyze if not destroy a system based on democracy.

In Africa and Latin America, Communist agents bearing substantial gifts in the form of economic aid have tried to win the allegiance of new governments. In Africa they have gone so far as to supply weapons and guerrilla training to insurgent groups. Elsewhere, infiltration of democratic regimes has succeeded in paralyzing parliamentary government and opening the way to Communist regimes.

For the Soviet leaders, each of these methods is costly. Guerrilla wars, as Vietnam has shown, can escalate to the brink of world conflict. Foreign aid requires diverting goods from undersupplied home markets. It is difficult to persuade the domestic consumer that he must sacrifice his needs for some faraway little brother in the jungle. But however costly, these weapons are all available and the Kremlin leaders have not hesitated to use them whenever there seemed to be a chance for success. The activities of undercover agents, infiltrators and subversionists in more advanced areas seriously undermine faith in the Kremlin's professions of "peaceful coexistence."

YET, in a way, such actions were forced on the Soviet leaders. Marxism-Leninism taught that the nations of the capitalist West would contribute to their own defeat by indulging in internecine "imperialist" wars, thus weakening themselves to the point where the workers could rise and upset their capitalist exploiters. But after World War II, contrary to Lenin's prognostications, the West, under American leadership, joined together first in the Marshall Plan to revive the economies of Europe and then in NATO to establish a common defense against the threat of Soviet military advance. Thanks in part to American economic aid and the American bomb, and in part to the united determination of the Western European states, the Soviet threat was contained and the Soviet armies remained more or less where they were when the war ended.

A combination of increasing affluence in the West and a lessening of the Soviet threat after Stalin's death eventually loosened the bonds of the Atlantic Community, but not before a much more fundamental split had taken place in the East.

Monolithic unity of the Communist world had been Stalin's watchword: a single eternal faith under a single infallible leader. In 1948

Tito had shaken this unity by breaking with Moscow and proclaiming that there were more paths than one to socialism. But the rest of the Communist world still hung together until Stalin died. Then Mao Tse-tung in Peking rejected Stalin's successors' claim to leadership and began to dispute their policies. The Eastern European Communist countries took advantage of the split to put national interests ahead of joint planning with Moscow and became less cooperative in COMECON (Council of Mutual Economic Assistance), the Soviet-sponsored instrument for economic integration among the members of the Soviet bloc. After the Sino-Soviet split, there no longer existed a unified worldwide Communist strategy.

No Church could long survive under two popes, and soon Mao was proclaiming that only Peking and its followers were truly Marxist. He even accused the Kremlin of betraying the entire movement by peacefully coexisting with the capitalist West, and his agents in Southeast Asia, Africa, Latin America and Western Europe openly fought the Kremlin's emissaries for control of the world Communist movement.

Inevitably, though perhaps reluctantly, the Soviet leaders were forced to defend their claim to leadership in the revolutionary movement by pursuing dangerously aggressive policies in Vietnam and elsewhere and by projecting a stultifying intransigence toward the West, particularly the United States, just at a time when their internal needs called for increasing cooperation and trade with the West.

IF unity is essential to the crusade for world domination, certainly a fervent faith in the crusade, at least at home, is equally important. Although one must presume that the older leaders in the Kremlin are devout believers in ultimate victory, there is increasing evidence that the once-enthusiastic masses who paraded endlessly through Red Square to demonstrate their faith in Communism are today apathetic if not downright skeptical that the promises held out to them for more than a generation will ever be fulfilled without fundamental modifications of the system. Few dream of supplanting the system. But equally few appear willing to risk further sacrifices, let alone war, to propagate it throughout the globe.

The jokes that circulate among the people are one of the better gauges of Soviet public opinion. In the early days of the Soviet regime they often reflected mild derision of the Kremlin leaders. Under Stalin they became so bitter that the dictator drove them underground. Today they are flourishing again. One of the favorite forms of political jokes is the supposed ineptness of a Soviet "Radio Armenia" in answering listeners' questions. For example, a listener asks: "Is it possible that France might one day go Communist?" "Yes, unfortunately," Radio Armenia replies.

BUT on one subject there is little joking: peace and war. If there is one aspiration that is common to every Soviet citizen it is "peace." The horrors, deprivations and losses in lives suffered during the German invasion are still fresh in everyone's mind. Any Kremlin action that the Soviet people regard as a threat to peace would find little support. But, by the same token, any action that appeared to constitute a threat of war by a foreign state would be universally condemned. For World War II not only made the longing for peace universal but also multiplied the natural Russian concern for national security. Indeed, some observers suggest that as enthusiasm for Marxism wanes, Russian nationalism tends to replace it.

In the last analysis, if the Kremlin leaders are to make any lasting progress in persuading the rest of the world, particularly the rising new states, to adopt their system, they must prove that it can work—not only in producing prodigious quantities of steel and weapons but in satisfying the minimum aspirations and needs of their citizens.

Here is the crux of the Soviet leaders' dilemma. How can they allocate their resources so as to satisfy the demands of the orthodox advocates of heavy industry, the vital needs of the defense establishment and the requirements of the space scientists, as well as the rising clamor of the consumer and the pitiful pleas of the peasantry? How can they adapt the dogma of central control to give plant managers and engineers the latitude they need to improve production methods and to give the economists the freedom they seek to devise planning, distributing and servicing systems workable in the complex, industrialized and newly plentiful economy that the Soviet Union today possesses? How can they satisfy the intellectuals—the writers and artists, the technologists and scientists —in their pleas for freedom to do their work as they think best and still not compromise the preordained right of the Communist Party to prescribe their very thoughts?

THE decentralizations and recentralizations, the shifting and reshifting of priorities, the recurrent rearguard actions against the intellectuals and the endless search for cheap panaceas for the farmers have indicated the need for fundamental changes. But the Marxist-Leninist system can be rigid and unadaptable to changing circumstances.

Nevertheless, in one important respect, the Soviet scene has changed. The cast of characters is different. In the long run every system of government is a reflection of the men who run it. Under Lenin the men who ran the Soviet system were mostly young, fanatical revolutionaries who had for the sake of their beliefs chosen between normal lives and those of outlaws. Inexperienced when they came to power, they governed by faith and expediency.

Under Stalin no one but he determined policy. His lieutenants were older, more practical men than Lenin's, utterly dominated by their fear of him. The men around Khrushchev were products of Stalin, who had trained them. Their experiences in the purges had made them cautious, wily and cunning. They were fearful of expressing original ideas, and they were hesitant about making innovations.

The top men today are mostly of the same generation and background as Khrushchev, but there are younger men, too, in the Presidium who were born after the Revolution. They did not choose Communism; they inherited it. By and large they are better educated than their older colleagues. They were too young to be as vulnerable as their elders to Stalin's terror and consequently today show self-confidence and candor in expressing their opinions. Most of them have traveled abroad and made acquaintances among Westerners. They are still young, still junior to the very top leaders, but they have risen fast and steadily, and today they are on the very threshold of supreme power. Their wartime experiences have made them fervent patriots. They seem less interested in propagating the Communist faith than they are in maintaining Russian prestige and power. Unlike Lenin's revolutionary followers, who had little to lose, they are the more careful heirs of the world's second industrial state.

Furthermore they are probably more aware than the older generation is of the aspirations of their fellow citizens, with whom they had contacts as teachers or youth-movement leaders not too long ago. Whatever their personal views and beliefs about Marxism may be, they certainly must be aware of the indifference to Marxist doctrines of their acquaintances in industry, the arts and sciences. They are all tough, rough, ruthless men. But one suspects that they are more cautious, less likely to risk their heritage for world revolution and for a dogma that has grown lusterless with age and has begun to reveal dispiriting flaws.

NO system can survive without change. Exactly how fast, how far and in what direction the new men will change it even they do not know. But that they face perhaps the gravest decisions in the history of the Soviet Union is clear. In all events, while the West awaits their decisions, there is no alternative policy for its statesmen to pursue but the ancient formula: "If you want peace, prepare for war."

"Everything has happened in Russia," an old European ambassador with years of experience in Moscow once remarked. "And," he added, "anything is likely to happen again."

*The modern Palace of Congresses, in the Kremlin beside the Troitskaya Tower, is lit for a session of the Communist Party Congress.*

SOVIET MIGHT *is maintained by an all-powerful regime . . .*

*Viktor Zharinov (center) celebrates his family's move to a new apartment in a big prefabricated development located outside Moscow.*

*. . . but the people, though proud of their nation's strength, are weary of*

*Formerly, Viktor, his wife, two young daughters and their grandmother shared two tiny rooms in a crumbling brick building.*

*revolutionary austerity and aspire to a more abundant, Western-style life*

# Appendix

## HISTORICAL DATES

| | |
|---|---|
| 862 | Traditional date for founding of Russian state. Varangians, warrior-merchants from Scandinavia led by Rurik the Viking, establish themselves at Novgorod. Start of Rurik dynasty |
| 882 | Varangians move south, occupying Kiev |
| 988 | Baptism of Vladimir I, Grand Prince of Kiev; Russian reception of Christianity |
| 1015-54 | Yaroslav the Wise inherits Novgorod, extends power over greater part of Russia. Kievan Russia attains peak of development |
| 1147 | First written mention of Moscow |
| 1223 | First appearance of Tatars; Battle of Kalka |
| 1237-40 | Tatar invasion of Russia |
| 1242 | Alexander Nevski, Grand Duke of Kiev and Novgorod, defeats Livonian knights |
| 1381 | Dmitri Donskoi, Grand Duke of Vladimir and Kiev, builder of the Kremlin, is defeated at Moscow by forces of Tamerlane |
| 1462-1505 | Reign of Ivan III (the Great) |
| 1472 | Ivan III marries Sophia, niece of last Byzantine Emperor; the marriage is important in establishing claim of Russian rulers as protectors of Orthodox Christianity |
| 1480 | Overthrow of Tatar rule by Ivan III |
| 1547 | Ivan IV (the Terrible) crowned Czar; first to use title formally |
| 1552-1556 | Ivan the Terrible conquers Kazan, takes Astrakhan |
| 1564 | First book printed in Moscow |
| 1581 | Ermak Timofeev sets out to conquer Siberia |
| 1589 | Establishment of Moscow patriarchate |
| 1598 | Rurik dynasty ends with death of Theodore, son of Ivan IV by his first wife, Anastasia Romanova |
| 1598-1605 | Boris Godunov elected to throne, reigns as Czar of Russia |
| 1598-1613 | "Time of Troubles": civil war, false claimants to throne, Cossack pillage and raids |
| 1613 | "Council of All the Russias" selects Michael Romanov, grandnephew of Ivan IV, as new Czar, beginning Romanov dynasty |
| 1639 | Russians reach the Pacific |
| 1667 | Russia obtains eastern Ukraine from Poland |
| 1689 | Russia's boundary with China fixed at the Amur River |
| 1703 | Founding of St. Petersburg by Peter I (the Great) |
| 1721 | Peter acquires Estonia and Livonia from Sweden |
| 1755 | University of Moscow founded: first Russian university |
| 1762-96 | Reign of Catherine II (the Great) |
| 1772-93 | First and Second Partitions of Poland add Byelorussia and most of western Ukraine |
| 1773-74 | Emelyan Pugachev leads peasant revolt |
| 1774 | Treaty with Turkey: free commercial navigation in Turkish waters; protection for Christian churches in Turkey |
| 1783 | First permanent Russian settlement in Alaska |
| 1792 | Turkey recognizes Russian annexation of the Crimea |
| 1795 | Third Partition of Poland adds Lithuania, Kurland and northwestern Ukraine |
| 1801-29 | Russia annexes Georgia and part of Armenia |
| 1809 | Sweden cedes Finland to Russia |
| 1812 | Napoleon invades Russia |
| 1815 | Congress of Vienna awards Russia control of Duchy of Warsaw |
| 1853-60 | Settlement of Pacific coastal lands |
| 1854-56 | Crimean War; Russia gives up claims to protectorate over the Orthodox in Turkey |
| 1861 | Alexander II emancipates the serfs |
| 1864-85 | Russia conquers Central Asia |
| 1867 | Russia sells Alaska to the U.S. |
| 1881 | Assassination of Alexander II |
| 1891 | Construction of Trans-Siberian Railroad begins |
| 1898 | First Convention of Marxist Social Democratic Party |
| 1905 | Russia defeated in Russo-Japanese War. The Revolution of 1905 |
| 1906 | Meeting of first Duma (Council of State) |
| 1914 | Start of World War I. Russia enters on side of Allies |

| 1917 | February Revolution. Abdication of Czar Nicholas II. October Revolution: Bolsheviks come to power |
|---|---|
| 1918 | Treaty of Brest-Litovsk ends Russian participation in World War I. Execution of Nicholas II |
| 1918-22 | Civil war; counterrevolution and foreign intervention; famine |
| 1919 | Founding of Communist International (Comintern) |
| 1921 | Introduction of New Economic Policy (NEP) |
| 1924 | Death of Lenin |
| 1927 | Trotsky expelled from Communist Party. Stalin supreme |
| 1929 | Intensive collectivization of farms begins |
| 1933 | United States recognizes the U.S.S.R. |
| 1936-38 | Stalin's purges |
| 1939 | Russia signs nonaggression pact with Germany. World War II begins. Russia annexes eastern Poland and invades Finland |
| 1940 | Russia annexes the Baltic states |
| 1941 | German invasion brings Russia into World War II |
| 1943 | Comintern dissolved |
| 1945 | World War II ends |
| 1948 | Communist coup in Czechoslovakia. Stalin breaks with Yugoslavia's Tito |
| 1948-49 | West Berlin blockaded by the Russians |
| 1950-53 | Korean War. Russia aids the North Koreans against United Nations forces |
| 1953 | Stalin's death |
| 1955 | Khrushchev effects reconciliation with Tito |
| 1956 | Poland's leadership changes. Hungary revolts |
| 1957 | Russia places first satellite in space |
| 1961 | At 22nd Soviet Communist Party Congress, Khrushchev attacks Stalinist "antiparty" group. Open rifts appear between Chinese and Soviet Communists |
| 1964 | Khrushchev ousted from power |

# REPUBLICS OF THE U.S.S.R.

The U.S.S.R. is made up of 14 Soviet Socialist Republics and one much larger unit, the Russian Soviet Federated Socialist Republic. Within the Russian Federation the major nationalities other than the Russian (mostly of Finnish, Turkish or Mongol origin) are subdivided into 13 Autonomous Soviet Socialist Republics, not listed here. The population figures at right are 1964 estimates.

| | CAPITAL | POPULATION | AREA (sq. mi.) |
|---|---|---|---|
| **Armenian Republic** | Yerevan | 2,072,000 | 11,306 |
| **Azerbaidzhan Republic** | Baku | 4,381,000 | 33,436 |
| **Byelorussian Republic** | Minsk | 8,454,000 | 80,154 |
| **Estonian Republic** | Tallin | 1,259,000 | 17,413 |
| **Georgian Republic** | Tbilisi | 4,410,000 | 26,911 |
| **Kazakh Republic** | Alma-Ata | 11,568,000 | 1,064,092 |
| **Kirgiz Republic** | Frunze | 2,488,000 | 76,642 |
| **Latvian Republic** | Riga | 2,210,000 | 24,695 |
| **Lithuanian Republic** | Vilnyus | 2,895,000 | 26,173 |
| **Moldavian Republic** | Kishinev | 3,245,000 | 13,012 |
| **Russian Republic** | Moscow | 124,777,000 | 6,593,391 |
| **Tadzhik Republic** | Dyushambe | 2,341,000 | 54,019 |
| **Turkmen Republic** | Ashkhabad | 1,803,000 | 188,417 |
| **Ukrainian Republic** | Kiev | 44,636,000 | 232,046 |
| **Uzbek Republic** | Tashkent | 9,714,000 | 158,069 |

# Notes

## FAMOUS RUSSIAN CULTURAL FIGURES AND THEIR PRINCIPAL WORKS

### LITERATURE

| | | |
|---|---|---|
| Pushkin, Aleksander | 1799-1837 | *Evgeni Onegin; Boris Godunov* |
| Gogol, Nikolai | 1809-1852 | *Dead Souls; The Inspector General* |
| Turgenev, Ivan | 1818-1883 | *Fathers and Sons; A Sportsman's Sketches* |
| Dostoevski, Fëdor | 1821-1881 | *Crime and Punishment; The Idiot; The Possessed; The Brothers Karamazov* |
| Tolstoi, Lev | 1828-1910 | *Anna Karenina; War and Peace* |
| Chekhov, Anton | 1860-1904 | *The Cherry Orchard; Uncle Vanya; The Three Sisters; The Sea Gull;* short stories |
| Gorki, Maxim | 1868-1936 | *My Childhood; Mother; The Lower Depths* |
| Blok, Aleksandr | 1880-1921 | Symbolist poet: *The Twelve* |
| Pasternak, Boris | 1890-1960 | *Doctor Zhivago;* selected poems |
| Sholokhov, Mikhail | 1905- | *And Quiet Flows the Don; Virgin Soil Upturned* |

### FINE ARTS

| | | |
|---|---|---|
| Rublev, Andreï | c.1360-1430 | Iconography: *The Trinity* |
| Bryulov, Karl | 1799-1852 | Painting: *The Last Day of Pompeii; Ascension of Christ* |
| Repin, Ilya | 1844-1930 | Painting: *Zaporozhe Cossacks Drafting a Reply to the Turkish Sultan* |
| Fabergé, Carl | 1846-1920 | Jewelry: enameled Easter eggs; jeweled birds and animals |
| Kandinsky, Vasili | 1866-1944 | Painting: Post-Impressionist; cofounder of the Abstract school |
| Chagall, Marc | 1889- | Painting: Expressionism |

## FOR FURTHER READING

### CHAPTERS 1, 2: LAND, PEOPLE, HISTORY

Brumberg, Abraham, ed., *Russia Under Khrushchev.* Frederick A. Praeger, 1962.

Carmichael, Joel, *A Short History of the Russian Revolution.* Basic Books, 1964.

Dallin, David J., *From Purge to Coexistence; Essays on Stalin's & Khrushchev's Russia.* Henry Regnery, 1964.

Fischer, Louis, *The Life of Lenin.* Harper & Row, 1964.

Kennan, George F., *Russia Leaves the War.* Princeton University Press, 1956. *Russia and the West Under Lenin and Stalin.* Little, Brown, 1961. *Soviet Foreign Policy, 1917-1941.* D. Van Nostrand, 1960.

Mosely, Philip E., ed., *The Soviet Union, 1922-1962; A Foreign Affairs Reader.* Frederick A. Praeger, 1963.

Riasanovsky, Nicholas V., *A History of Russia.* Oxford University Press, 1963.

Seton-Watson, Hugh, *From Lenin to Khrushchev; The History of World Communism.* Frederick A. Praeger, 1960.

Wolfe, Bertram D., *Marxism: One Hundred Years in the Life of a Doctrine.* Dial Press, 1965.

### CHAPTER 3: POLITICS

Brzezinski, Zbigniew, and Samuel P. Huntington, *Political Power: USA/USSR.* Viking, 1964.

Fainsod, Merle, *How Russia Is Ruled.* Harvard University Press, rev. ed., 1963.

Hazard, John N., *The Soviet System of Government.* University of Chicago Press, 3rd ed., 1964.

Leonhard, Wolfgang, *The Kremlin Since Stalin.* Frederick A. Praeger, 1962.

Pethybridge, Roger, *A Key to Soviet Politics; The Crisis of the Anti-Party Group.* Frederick A. Praeger, 1962.

### CHAPTERS 4, 5: THE ECONOMY

Agricultural Research Service. *Soviet Agriculture Today; Report of the 1963 Agriculture Exchange Delegation.* United States Department of Agriculture, 1964.

Bergson, Abram, and Simon Kuznets, *Economic Trends in the Soviet Union.* Harvard University Press, 1963.

Campbell, Robert W., *Soviet Economic Power; Its Organization, Growth, and Challenge.* Houghton Mifflin, 1960.

Dobb, Maurice, *Soviet Economic Development Since 1917.* International Publishers, 1948.

Lydolf, Paul E., *Geography of the U.S.S.R.* John Wiley and Sons, 1964.

Nove, Alec, *The Soviet Economy; An Introduction.* Frederick A. Praeger, 1961.

Schwartz, Harry, *Russia's Soviet Economy.* Prentice-Hall, 2nd ed., 1958. *The Soviet Economy Since Stalin.* J. B. Lippincott, 1965.

Volin, Lazar, *A Survey of Soviet Russian Agriculture.* U.S. Government Printing Office, 1951.

### CHAPTERS 6, 9: LIVING CONDITIONS, LEISURE

Black, Cyril E., ed., *The Transformation of Russian Society;*

## MUSIC

| | | |
|---|---|---|
| Borodin, Aleksandr | 1834-1887 | *In the Steppes of Central Asia; Prince Igor* |
| Musorgski, Modest | 1835-1881 | *Boris Godunov; Pictures at an Exhibition; Night on Bald Mountain* |
| Tchaikovsky, Pëtr | 1840-1893 | *Symphonies Nos. 4, 5, 6; Piano Concerto No. 1; Nutcracker Suite; Swan Lake* |
| Rimski-Korsakov, Nikolai | 1844-1908 | *Scheherazade; Le Coq d'Or; Ivan the Terrible; The Snow Maiden* |
| Rachmaninoff, Sergei | 1873-1943 | *Piano Concerto No. 2; Symphony No. 2; Prelude in C Sharp Minor* |
| Stravinsky, Igor | 1882- | *The Fire Bird; Petrouchka; The Rite of Spring* |
| Prokofiev, Sergei | 1891-1953 | *Peter and the Wolf; Classical Symphony; The Love for Three Oranges* |
| Khachaturyan, Aram | 1903- | *Masquerade; Gayne* |
| Shostakovich, Dmitri | 1906- | *Symphonies Nos. 1, 5, 7; The Nose; Lady Macbeth of Mtsensk* |

## PERFORMING ARTS

| | | |
|---|---|---|
| Stanislavski, Konstantin | 1863-1938 | Cofounder of the Moscow Art Theater; innovator of "method" school of acting |
| Chaliapin, Feodor | 1873-1938 | Operatic basso who was outstanding in *Boris Godunov* and *Mefistofele* |
| Meyerhold, Vsevolod | 1874-1940 | Theatrical producer; creator of Russian modernist theater |
| Pavlova, Anna | 1885-1931 | Prima ballerina famous as *The Dying Swan* |
| Nijinsky, Waslaw | 1890-1950 | Premier danseur who was the first to dance *The Afternoon of a Faun* |
| Oistrakh, David | 1908- | Concert violinist |
| Ulanova, Galina | 1910- | Prima ballerina of the Bolshoi Ballet, outstanding in *Swan Lake* |
| Richter, Sviatoslav | 1914- | Concert pianist |
| Gilels, Emil | 1916- | Concert pianist |

*Aspects of Social Change Since 1861.* Harvard University Press, 1960.

Feifer, George, *Justice in Moscow.* Simon and Schuster, 1964.

Fischer, Markoosha, *Reunion in Moscow.* Harper & Row, 1962.

Inkeles, Alex, and Kent Geiger, eds., *Soviet Society; A Book of Readings.* Houghton Mifflin, 1961.

Salisbury, Harrison, *A New Russia?* Harper & Row, 1962.

Sillitoe, Alan, *Road to Volgograd.* Alfred A. Knopf, 1964.

Van der Post, Laurens, *A View of All the Russias.* Morrow, 1964.

## CHAPTER 7: EDUCATION AND RELIGION

Fischer, George, *Science and Politics; the New Sociology in the Soviet Union.* Cornell University, 1964.

Kolarz, Walter, *Religion in the Soviet Union.* St Martin's Press, 1962.

Spinka, Matthew, *The Church in Soviet Russia.* Oxford University Press, 1956.

Whiting, Kenneth R., *The Soviet Union Today; A Concise Handbook.* Frederick A. Praeger, 1962.

## CHAPTER 8: ARTS AND LETTERS

Alexandrova, Vera, *A History of Soviet Literature.* Doubleday, 1963.

Blake, Patricia, and Max Hayward, eds., *Half-way to the Moon; New Writing From Russia.* Holt, Rinehart and Winston, 1964.

Bowers, Faubion, *Broadway, U.S.S.R.; Ballet, Theatre and Entertainment in Russia Today.* Nelson, 1959.

Hamilton, George Heard, *The Art and Architecture of Russia.* Penguin Books, 1954.

Hayward, Max, and Edward L. Crowley, eds., *Soviet Literature in the Sixties.* Frederick A. Praeger, 1964.

Reavey, George, ed., *Modern Soviet Short Stories.* Grosset & Dunlap, 1961.

Slonim, Marc, *Modern Russian Literature; From Chekhov to the Present.* Oxford University Press, 1953. *Soviet Russian Literature; Writers and Problems.* Oxford University Press, 1964.

Spector, Ivar, *An Introduction to Russian History and Culture.* D. Van Nostrand, 3rd ed., 1961.

## CHAPTER 10: TRENDS

Braverman, Harry, *The Future of Russia.* Macmillan, 1963.

Conquest, Robert, *Russia After Khrushchev.* Frederick A. Praeger, 1965.

Dallin, Alexander, and others, *The Soviet Union, Arms Control, and Disarmament; A Study of Soviet Attitudes.* Columbia University, 1964.

Harcave, Sidney, *Russia A History.* J. B. Lippincott, 1964.

Lowenthal, Richard, *World Communism, the Disintegration of a Secular Faith.* Oxford University Press, 1964.

Schwartz, Harry, *Tsars, Mandarins, and Commissars; A History of Chinese-Russian Relations.* J. B. Lippincott, 1964.

Zagoria, Donald S., *The Sino-Soviet Conflict, 1956-1961.* Princeton University Press, 1962.

# Credits

*The sources for the illustrations in this book appear below. Credits for pictures from left to right are separated by commas, from top to bottom by dashes.*

Cover—Howard Sochurek
8—James Whitmore
17—Gregory Shuker
18, 19—Howard Sochurek except bottom right Gregory Shuker
20, 21—Carl Mydans
22, 23—Stan Wayman, Howard Sochurek
24, 25—Howard Sochurek
26, 27—John Launois from Black Star except right Howard Sochurek
28—Painting by Morton Roberts
37—Herbert Orth courtesy Prince Serge Belosselsky
38 through 43—David Douglas Duncan
44—Carl Mydans
45—Rune Hassner from Gamma
46—John Dominis—Photo CAF—United Press International Cablephoto from TASS
47, 48, 49—Sovfoto
51—Diagram by The Chartmakers, Inc.
55—Sovfoto
56—Howard Sochurek
57—Howard Sochurek—USSR from Sovfoto
58—Left: Sovfoto—Stan Wayman
60, 61—James Whitmore
65, 66—Charts by Matt Greene
69—Dan Weiner for FORTUNE
70, 71—Howard Sochurek—Stan Wayman, Howard Sochurek

72—Jerry Cooke for TIME
73—Stan Wayman—James Whitmore—Stan Wayman
74, 75—Left: John Launois from Black Star; center: James Whitmore—Stan Wayman; right: Howard Sochurek
76, 77—Left: Howard Sochurek—Stan Wayman; right: Wide World Photos
78, 79—Margaret Bourke-White
83—Chart by Matt Greene
85—Howard Sochurek
86, 87—Left: Herb Plambeck, Stan Wayman—Howard Sochurek; right: Stan Wayman
88—Stan Wayman
89—Howard Sochurek
90, 91—Left: John Launois from Black Star; right: Stan Wayman
92—Dan Weiner for FORTUNE
93—Lisa Larsen
94—Dan Weiner for FORTUNE
103, 104, 105—Howard Sochurek
106, 107—Stan Wayman except right Agence Dalmas
108, 109—Stan Wayman
110—Elliott Erwitt from Magnum
117, 118, 119—Cornell Capa from Magnum
120—Bruce Davidson from Magnum
121—Stan Wayman
122, 123—Henri Cartier-Bresson from Magnum

124, 125—Stan Wayman
126, 127—Dan Weiner—Howard Sochurek
128—Dan Weiner
134—Jerry Cooke except top right TASS
135—Edward Clark
136—Howard Sochurek—Leonard McCombe
137—Cornell Capa from Magnum
138, 139—John Bryson, Alexander Marshack
140—Marilyn Silverstone from Nancy Palmer Photo Agency—Elliott Erwitt from Magnum
141—Edward Clark
142, 143—Howard Sochurek
144—Jerry Cooke for SPORTS ILLUSTRATED
150, 151—Stan Wayman
152, 153—Lisa Larsen, Jerry Cooke for SPORTS ILLUSTRATED
154, 155—Left: Jerry Cooke for SPORTS ILLUSTRATED; center: Larry Burrows—Howard Sochurek; right: Jerry Cooke for SPORTS ILLUSTRATED
156—Yuri Korolev for SPORTS ILLUSTRATED
157—Jerry Cooke for SPORTS ILLUSTRATED
158, 159—Carl Mydans
160—Dan Weiner for FORTUNE
165—James Whitmore
166, 167—Stan Wayman

## ACKNOWLEDGMENTS

The following scholars were of assistance to the editors: Philip E. Mosely, Director of Studies for the Council on Foreign Relations, and George Fischer, Department of Sociology, Columbia University, both of whom read and commented on the entire text; Joseph S. Berliner of the Department of Economics, Syracuse University, who helped on Chapters 4 through 6; George Z. F. Bereday of Teachers College, Columbia University, who provided education information; Maurice Friedberg, Russian Division, Hunter College, who gave guidance on literature; and Cyril E. Black, Department of History, Princeton University, who gave assistance on Russo-Chinese relations.

# Index

*This symbol in front of a page number indicates a photograph or painting of the subject mentioned.*

✗✗✗✗✗

*Production staff for Time Incorporated*

*John L. Hallenbeck (Vice President and Director of Production)*

*Robert E. Foy, Caroline Ferri and Robert E. Fraser*

*Text photocomposed under the direction of*

*Albert J. Dunn and Arthur J. Dunn*

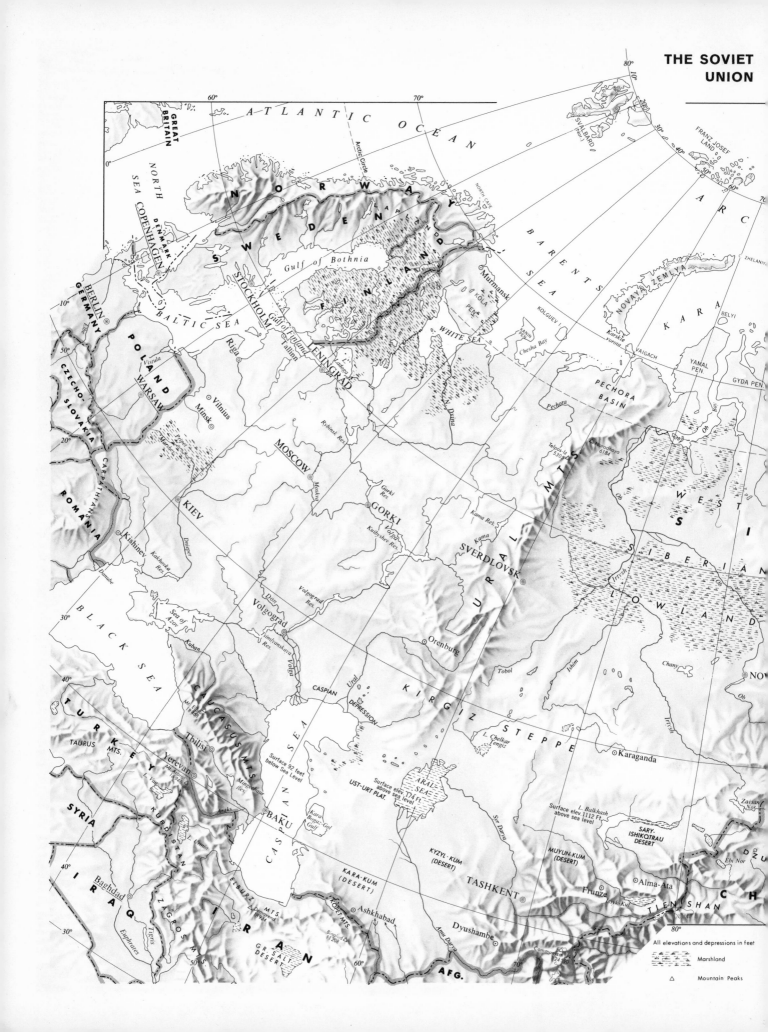

# THE SOVIET UNION

All elevations and depressions in feet

Marshland

△ Mountain Peaks